The Rigid and Controlling Marriage

A Partner's Guide to OCPD, Boundaries, and Reclaiming Your Life

Willard Mario Nixon

Copyright © 2025 by Willard Mario Nixon

All rights reserved. No part of this publication may be reproduced, distributed, or transmitted in any form or by any means, including photocopying, recording, or other electronic or mechanical methods, without the prior written permission of the publisher, except in the case of brief quotations embodied in critical reviews and certain other noncommercial uses permitted by copyright law.

First Edition

ISBN :9781923604506

This book is intended for informational and educational purposes only. It is not a substitute for professional psychological, psychiatric, or medical advice, diagnosis, or treatment. The content provided in this book does not constitute a therapeutic relationship.

Always seek the advice of your physician or other qualified health provider with any questions you may have regarding a medical or mental health condition. If you are experiencing distress, relationship abuse, or a crisis, please seek the assistance of a qualified healthcare professional immediately. Never disregard professional medical advice or delay in seeking it because of something you have read in this book.

The author and publisher specifically disclaim any liability, loss, or risk, personal or otherwise, which is incurred as a consequence, directly or indirectly, of the use and application of any of the contents of this book.

Case examples and scenarios presented in this book are amalgamations of common experiences or are used fictitiously. All names, characters, and incidents portrayed are illustrative composites. Any resemblance to actual persons, living or dead, or actual events is purely coincidental.

Table of Contents

Chapter 1: Is It Perfectionism, or Is It OCPD? 1

Chapter 2: The Crucial Distinction: OCPD vs. OCD 10

Chapter 3: The Hallmarks of the OCPD Spouse 18

Chapter 4: What Drives the Control? The Hidden Anxiety 26

Chapter 5: Walking on Eggshells: The Emotional Toll 35

Chapter 6: The Loneliest Marriage 44

Chapter 7: Recognizing Control and Manipulation Tactics 52

Chapter 8: When Control Crumbles: Anger Outbursts and Rage 59

Chapter 9: The Essential First Step: Boundaries, Not Battles 66

Chapter 10: De-escalation and Effective Communication 76

Chapter 11: Navigating the Daily Grind: Specific Pain Points 85

Chapter 12: Reclaiming Your Identity: Radical Self-Care 93

Chapter 13: Can an OCPD Person Change? 101

Chapter 14: Therapy and Intervention 108

Chapter 15: The Decision Point: Knowing When to Walk Away 115

Conclusion: Your Life, Your Rules 121

Appendix A: OCPD Symptom Checklist 124

Appendix B: Boundary Setting Worksheet and Scripts 126

Appendix C: Resources 128

Appendix D: A Letter to the OCPD Partner 130

Reference 132

Chapter 1: Is It Perfectionism, or Is It OCPD?

It often starts small. Maybe your partner reorganized the pantry again because you didn't stack the cans with the labels facing perfectly forward. Perhaps they "helped" you by refolding the laundry because your method wasn't efficient enough. When you first met, you probably admired their dedication. They seemed organized, driven, and had incredibly high standards. They seemed to have it all together.

But somewhere along the line, that helpful organization turned into rigid control. Their high standards stopped feeling motivational and started feeling like a constant judgment. You might find yourself second-guessing every small decision you make—from how you chop an onion to how you schedule your day—because you know there's a "right way" and a "wrong way" to do things. And your way, increasingly, seems to be the wrong way.

This feeling of constantly falling short is exhausting. It makes you wonder, "Why are they like this? Why is nothing ever good enough?" You might assume they are just a perfectionist or maybe a bit of a "control freak." But what if it's something more?

This brings us to Obsessive-Compulsive Personality Disorder, or OCPD. It's a term that gets thrown around sometimes, often incorrectly. Understanding what OCPD truly is, and whether it fits your partner's behavior, is the first step in changing how you manage your relationship. This isn't about labeling your spouse; it's about understanding the framework they operate within so you can stop feeling so confused and overwhelmed.

Defining Obsessive-Compulsive Personality Disorder

Let's clear something up right away: OCPD is not just about liking things neat. It's a personality disorder. Now, that term sounds serious, but let's break down what it actually means.

A personality disorder isn't an illness that flares up and then goes away, like the flu. It's an enduring pattern of inner experience and outward behavior. It deviates markedly from the expectations of the individual's culture (American Psychiatric Association, 2022). In simpler terms, it's the lens through which a person views the world, affecting how they think, feel, and relate to others. This pattern is **inflexible** and pervasive across a broad range of situations. It's not something they can just turn off.

For someone with OCPD, their personality is structured around a profound need for orderliness, perfectionism, and mental and interpersonal control. They need this control to feel functional. The problem is, the world is not perfectly ordered, and other people cannot be perfectly controlled. This clash between their internal needs and external reality is where the conflict in your marriage happens.

The crucial thing to understand about OCPD—and this is really important—is that the individual usually does not see their behavior as a problem. They see it as the correct, logical, and most efficient way to live. When conflict arises, they genuinely believe that if everyone else (meaning you) would just do things the "right way," everything would be fine.

OCPD is actually one of the most common personality disorders. Some estimates suggest that it may affect up to 7.9% of the population (American Psychiatric Association, 2022). That means millions of people are navigating life with this rigid framework, and millions more are trying to love them. You are definitely not alone in this struggle.

The Key Traits: Preoccupation with Orderliness, Perfectionism, and Interpersonal Control

OCPD revolves around three main themes. Think of these as the pillars that hold up the OCPD worldview.

The Preoccupation with Orderliness

When we talk about orderliness in OCPD, we aren't just talking about a clean house. We are talking about a mental preoccupation with rules, lists, details, schedules, and organization. The focus on the *process* is so intense that the actual point of the activity often gets lost.

For example, your partner might decide to organize the garage. A typical person wants the garage organized so they can easily find their tools. A person with OCPD might spend hours creating a detailed inventory system, labeling every single screw, and drawing a map of where everything should go. They might become so focused on the system of organization that they never actually finish organizing the garage. The process of creating order becomes the goal, rather than the result.

This rigidity often shows up in how they manage time. Spontaneity is very difficult for someone with OCPD. They often feel a strong need to schedule everything, even leisure activities. A vacation might be planned down to 15-minute increments. If something disrupts the schedule—say, traffic causes a delay—it doesn't just cause annoyance; it can cause genuine distress or even anger. The disruption of the order feels catastrophic.

The Debilitating Perfectionism

We often value perfectionism. But the perfectionism in OCPD is different. It's *maladaptive perfectionism*—it actually interferes with getting things done.

The standards they set for themselves, and often for you, are unrealistically high. They are so afraid of making a mistake that they may procrastinate or become paralyzed, unable to finish a project because it isn't "perfect" yet. They might spend hours rewriting a simple email to make sure the wording is exactly right, missing the deadline in the process.

This perfectionism also extends to morality and ethics. People with OCPD are often overly conscientious, scrupulous, and inflexible about matters of morality, ethics, or values (American Psychiatric Association, 2022). They see the world in black and white. There is a right way and a wrong way, with no gray area in between.

This can be incredibly difficult in a marriage because relationships require flexibility. If your partner views a disagreement not just as a difference of opinion, but as a moral failing on your part, it's very hard to find common ground.

The Need for Interpersonal Control

This is often the most damaging trait within a relationship. The need for order and perfection doesn't just apply to their own lives; it extends to the people around them.

People with OCPD have a very hard time delegating tasks or working with others unless those others submit exactly to their way of doing things (American Psychiatric Association, 2022). If they ask you to help with a task, they might hover over you, correcting you constantly, or simply take over and do it themselves because they don't trust you to do it correctly.

This isn't necessarily because they want to be mean. It stems from a genuine belief that their method is superior and the only way to achieve the desired outcome. They believe they are helping you by showing you the "right way."

This control often manifests as stubbornness and rigidity. Once they have decided on something, it is nearly impossible to change their mind. They will present logical arguments for why their way is best, and they will dismiss your perspective as illogical or inefficient. They are trying to control the environment and the people in it to reduce their own anxiety about potential chaos or errors.

Checklists and Diagnostic Criteria (Simplified for the Layperson)

In the world of psychology, we use the *Diagnostic and Statistical Manual of Mental Disorders* (DSM-5-TR) to diagnose conditions like OCPD. A formal diagnosis requires a pervasive pattern of preoccupation with orderliness, perfectionism, and mental and interpersonal control, at the expense of flexibility, openness, and efficiency (American Psychiatric Association, 2022).

To meet the criteria, an individual must exhibit at least four out of the following eight traits.

1. **Is preoccupied with details, rules, lists, order, organization, or schedules to the extent that the major point of the activity is lost.**
   - *What this looks like:* Spending hours planning a family outing but having no fun during the outing because they are so focused on sticking to the schedule.

2. **Shows perfectionism that interferes with task completion.**
   - *What this looks like:* Being unable to finish a report because it is not yet "good enough." Repeatedly cleaning an already clean kitchen because they see microscopic flaws.

3. **Is excessively devoted to work and productivity to the exclusion of leisure activities and friendships (not accounted for by economic necessity).**
   - *What this looks like:* Consistently working late, even when not required. Viewing hobbies or relaxation as a "waste of time."

4. **Is overconscientious, scrupulous, and inflexible about matters of morality, ethics, or values (not accounted for by cultural or religious identification).**

- *What this looks like:* Rigidly adhering to rules, even when bending them would be harmless. Being extremely judgmental of others who make mistakes. A strong sense of "should" and "must."

5. **Is unable to discard worn-out or worthless objects even when they have no sentimental value.**
    - *What this looks like:* Hoarding items "just in case" they might be needed someday. Saving old newspapers or broken appliances. This is about control over resources, not emotional attachment.

6. **Is reluctant to delegate tasks or to work with others unless they submit to exactly his or her way of doing things.**
    - *What this looks like:* Refusing to let you help with cooking because you "do it wrong." Micromanaging every detail.

7. **Adopts a miserly spending style toward both self and others; money is viewed as something to be hoarded for future catastrophes.**
    - *What this looks like:* Extreme frugality, living well below their means, and becoming anxious about spending money, even on necessities. Arguing over small expenses.

8. **Shows rigidity and stubbornness.**
    - *What this looks like:* An inability to compromise. Insisting that their perspective is the only correct one. Becoming extremely defensive when criticized.

Remember, having one or two of these traits doesn't mean a person has OCPD. We all have moments of rigidity. OCPD is diagnosed when these traits are pervasive (they happen all the time), persistent (they have been happening for a long time), and pathological (they cause significant distress or impairment in relationships or work) (American Psychiatric Association, 2022).

The Difference Between High Standards and Pathological Rigidity

This is where many partners get confused. They might say, "But isn't it good to have high standards?" Yes, it is. But there is a clear line between healthy conscientiousness and OCPD.

The difference lies in **flexibility** and the **impact** of the behavior.

Flexibility vs. Inflexibility

A person with high standards can adjust their expectations based on the situation. They understand that sometimes "good enough" is acceptable if it means meeting a deadline or preserving a relationship. They value the outcome more than the process.

A person with OCPD struggles intensely with flexibility. Their standards are rigid and must be met regardless of the context. They value the process—doing it the "right way"—more than the outcome. If the situation demands a change in approach, they become anxious and resistant.

Case Example: The Dinner Party

Sarah has high standards. She is hosting a dinner party and plans an elaborate menu. Halfway through cooking, the oven breaks. Sarah is stressed, but she adapts. She switches gears, orders high-quality takeout, plates it nicely, and focuses on enjoying her guests' company. Her priority is the social connection.

Mark has OCPD. He is hosting a dinner party. If the oven breaks, Mark is likely to spiral. He cannot accept the idea of serving food he did not prepare exactly according to his plan. He might become irritable and angry, unable to socialize because he is preoccupied with the failure of the meal. He might even cancel the party because if he can't do it perfectly, he won't do it at all. His priority is the perfect execution of the plan.

Efficiency vs. Inefficiency

High standards often lead to efficiency. People who are organized get things done effectively.

Ironically, OCPD often leads to *inefficiency*. The preoccupation with details, the procrastination due to fear of mistakes, and the time spent checking and rechecking work mean that people with OCPD often take much longer to complete tasks than others. They get lost in the minutiae. They are busy, but not always productive.

Connection vs. Control

A healthy individual values relationships and connection. They understand that compromise and empathy are necessary for a healthy marriage.

A person with OCPD prioritizes control and correctness above connection. They struggle to compromise because they believe their way is the only right way. They may view emotions as messy or illogical, interfering with the efficient running of the household.

Understanding the Impact on You

If you are living with someone who exhibits these traits, life can feel like a constant performance review. You may feel criticized, controlled, and emotionally disconnected. You might start to doubt your own competence and judgment.

It's important to recognize that their behavior is not a reflection of your worth. It is a manifestation of their personality disorder. Their need for control stems from a deep internal rigidity, not from your inadequacy.

Recognizing the pattern is the first step. Once you see that these behaviors are connected and driven by OCPD, you can stop taking it so personally.

But before we go deeper into the behaviors of the OCPD spouse, we need to address a major point of confusion. When people hear

"Obsessive-Compulsive," they often think of OCD. But OCPD and OCD are fundamentally different, and understanding that difference is key to understanding why your partner acts the way they do.

Points to Remember

- OCPD is a personality disorder characterized by an enduring, inflexible pattern of preoccupation with orderliness, perfectionism, and control.

- It is not just about being neat; it is about a rigidity that impairs functioning and relationships.

- The key traits include excessive focus on details, perfectionism that hinders task completion, excessive devotion to work, inflexibility, difficulty discarding objects, reluctance to delegate, miserly spending habits, and stubbornness.

- Healthy conscientiousness involves flexibility and valuing connection. OCPD involves inflexibility and prioritizing control over connection.

- Recognizing these patterns in your partner is the first step toward understanding the dynamics of your relationship.

Chapter 2: The Crucial Distinction: OCPD vs. OCD

If you've started talking to friends or family about your partner's behavior—the rigid routines, the need for everything to be "just so"—you've probably heard someone say, "Oh, they sound so OCD." It's a phrase that's become part of our everyday language, often used casually to describe someone who is neat or organized.

And when you look at the names—Obsessive-Compulsive Personality Disorder (OCPD) and Obsessive-Compulsive Disorder (OCD)—they sound almost identical. It's natural to assume they are related. But here's the truth: OCPD and OCD are fundamentally different disorders.

Confusing the two can lead to significant misunderstandings about what your partner is experiencing and how you should respond. If you approach your OCPD partner as if they have OCD, your efforts to help or communicate will likely fail, leaving you both feeling more frustrated and disconnected.

Understanding this distinction is crucial. It explains why your partner resists help, why they blame you for problems, and why traditional relationship advice often doesn't work.

The Fundamental Difference: Anxiety vs. Values

While both disorders involve "obsessive" and "compulsive" elements, the nature of those elements is entirely different.

OCD: Driven by Irrational Anxiety

OCD is fundamentally an anxiety disorder. People with OCD experience *obsessions*, which are intrusive, unwanted, and distressing thoughts, images, or urges. These often center around themes of contamination, harm, or the need for symmetry. For example, an intense fear of germs, or a recurring thought that they left the stove on and the house will burn down.

To relieve the anxiety caused by these obsessions, people with OCD engage in *compulsions*. These are repetitive behaviors or mental acts. Examples include excessive hand washing, checking locks repeatedly, counting, or arranging objects in a specific way.

The key characteristic of OCD is that the individual usually recognizes that their obsessions and compulsions are irrational and excessive. They don't *want* to spend hours washing their hands. They know that checking the lock 20 times is illogical. But the anxiety is so intense that they feel compelled to perform the rituals anyway. The behaviors are driven by a fear of something terrible happening if they don't.

OCPD: Driven by Values and Beliefs

OCPD, on the other hand, is a personality disorder. It is not primarily driven by irrational fears, but by a deeply ingrained belief system centered on order, perfectionism, and control.

People with OCPD do not have intrusive, unwanted thoughts in the same way. Their "obsessions" are preoccupations with rules, details, efficiency, and correctness. They think constantly about how things "should" be done.

Their "compulsions" are not rituals performed to relieve anxiety about a specific fear. They are behaviors aimed at achieving perfection and maintaining order. This includes making lists, organizing excessively, and adhering rigidly to routines.

Unlike people with OCD, people with OCPD believe their behaviors are rational, logical, and correct. They *want* to be organized and perfect. They value these traits and believe that everyone else should too.

Why the Confusion Matters in Relationships

The confusion between OCD and OCPD can have significant consequences for your marriage.

Understanding the Motivation

If you believe your partner has OCD, you might assume their behaviors are driven by anxiety. You might try to reassure them, saying, "It's okay, the house is clean enough."

But if your partner has OCPD, their behavior is driven by a belief that their way is the *only correct way*. When you tell them "it's clean enough," they hear, "You don't care about doing things properly." Your reassurance feels like a dismissal of their values.

Understanding that OCPD is driven by a rigid belief system helps you recognize why logical arguments and reassurance don't work. You are not just arguing about chores; you are arguing about fundamental values.

Recognizing the Impact on Connection

People with OCD often feel distressed by their symptoms. They may feel guilty or ashamed of their compulsions. They are often willing to seek help to reduce their symptoms and improve their connections with others.

People with OCPD, however, often view their traits as strengths. They see themselves as responsible and reliable. They may view their partner's more relaxed attitude as lazy or irresponsible. They are more likely to try to change their partner than to change themselves.

In an OCPD marriage, the focus is often on performance rather than emotional connection. The OCPD individual may struggle to express warmth and affection because emotions are messy. They prioritize control over intimacy.

The Crucial Concept: Ego-Dystonic vs. Ego-Syntonic

The most important distinction between OCD and OCPD lies in how the individual views their own symptoms. This is where we get into two psychological terms that sound complicated but are actually quite simple: *ego-dystonic* and *ego-syntonic*. Understanding these terms is a game-changer.

OCD (Ego-Dystonic): The Unwelcome Intruder

Ego-dystonic means that the thoughts and behaviors are inconsistent with the individual's self-concept and values. They are dissonant, or out of tune, with who the person wants to be.

In OCD, the symptoms are ego-dystonic. The person experiences their obsessions and compulsions as intrusive and distressing. They are aware that their behavior is irrational. They often feel tormented by their symptoms and wish they could stop.

Think of it like having a pebble in your shoe. You know it's there, it's uncomfortable, and you want it gone. The pebble is separate from you.

Case Example: Maria's Struggle with OCD

Maria has OCD with contamination fears. She is terrified of germs and feels compelled to wash her hands repeatedly. Her hands are raw and cracked. Maria hates this. She knows her fear is excessive. She feels ashamed of her behavior and desperately wants help. When her husband expresses concern, she feels understood and supported. Her symptoms are ego-dystonic.

OCPD (Ego-Syntonic): The "Right Way" to Be

Ego-syntonic means that the thoughts and behaviors are consistent with the individual's self-concept and values. They are in tune with who the person believes they are.

In OCPD, the symptoms are ego-syntonic. The person views their preoccupation with order and control as rational, desirable, and correct. They identify with these traits and see them as strengths. They genuinely believe that their way is the best way, and that others are the ones with the problem.

Think of it this way: They don't see a pebble in their shoe. They believe their shoes are the most efficient, logical, and superior shoes available, and they cannot understand why everyone else is wearing such disorganized footwear.

Case Example: David's OCPD Mindset

David has OCPD. He spends hours organizing his workspace, making sure every item is perfectly aligned. He has strict routines for everything. He believes his methods are efficient and logical. When his wife tries to help with chores, he corrects her constantly, explaining why her method is inferior. He feels proud of his organization and frustrated by his wife's "sloppiness." When his wife suggests he is too rigid, he becomes defensive and lists all the reasons why his way is superior. His symptoms are ego-syntonic.

The Impact of Ego-Syntonic Beliefs

The ego-syntonic nature of OCPD is the core reason why it is so difficult to live with. It creates a dynamic where the OCPD individual genuinely believes they are right and everyone else is wrong.

The Belief That Others Are the Problem

When conflict arises, the OCPD individual does not look inward and think, "Maybe I am being too rigid." Instead, they look outward and think, "Why is my partner so incompetent?" They genuinely believe that the problems in the relationship are caused by their partner's failure to meet their standards.

This can be incredibly damaging to your self-esteem. You are constantly being told that you are the problem, and over time, you may start to believe it

The Inability to Compromise

Compromise requires the ability to see the validity of another person's perspective. But for someone with OCPD, there is no middle ground. There is the right way (their way) and the wrong way (your way).

When you ask them to compromise, they don't see it as a reasonable request. They see it as asking them to sacrifice their standards or to intentionally do something incorrectly. They will resist compromise fiercely. They are not just being stubborn; they are defending what they believe to be the truth.

The Lack of Empathy

People with OCPD often struggle with empathy, not because they are cold, but because their rigid thinking makes it difficult for them to understand why others feel differently than they do (Diedrich & Voderholzer, 2015). They may dismiss your feelings as illogical or overly sensitive.

If you tell them, "I feel hurt when you criticize the way I do the laundry," they might respond with, "I'm not criticizing you, I'm just showing you the correct way to fold the towels. If you did it right, I wouldn't have to correct you." They cannot understand why you would feel hurt by what they see as helpful instruction.

Why OCPD Individuals Rarely Seek Help on Their Own

The ego-syntonic nature of OCPD is also the main reason why individuals with this disorder rarely seek help on their own. Why would you seek help for something you don't see as a problem?

Think back to the pebble in the shoe. If you have a pebble (ego-dystonic), you are motivated to remove it. You want relief.

But if you believe your shoes are perfect (ego-syntonic), you are not motivated to change them. If someone suggests you change your shoes, you would likely become defensive.

People with OCPD usually only end up in therapy if they are pressured by others, often because their marriage is falling apart. They may come to therapy to complain about their partner, seeking validation that they are right and everyone else is wrong.

The "Gift" of Crisis

Sometimes, a crisis can crack open the OCPD defense system. When their rigid adherence to rules leads to a significant failure—such as losing a job or their partner threatening to leave—they may be forced to confront the reality that their way is not working.

This crisis can sometimes create a window of opportunity for change. However, this requires a significant amount of self-reflection and a willingness to challenge their deeply held beliefs, which is very difficult for someone with OCPD.

What This Means for You

Understanding the distinction between OCD and OCPD, and the ego-syntonic nature of OCPD, is crucial for your survival in this relationship.

Stop Trying to Convince Them They Are Wrong

When you realize that their beliefs are ego-syntonic, you can stop wasting your energy trying to convince them that they are wrong. They genuinely cannot see it. Arguing with them about the "right way" to do things is futile. It only leads to frustration and conflict.

Instead of focusing on changing their mind, focus on setting boundaries around their behavior.

Recognize That Their Behavior Is Not About You

Their criticism and control are not a reflection of your competence or worth. They are manifestations of their internal rigidity. When they correct you, they are not intentionally trying to hurt you (usually); they are trying to uphold their internal standards.

This doesn't excuse the behavior, but it can help you take it less personally.

Adjust Your Expectations

If you are hoping that your partner will suddenly wake up one day and realize they have been wrong, you are likely to be disappointed. Change for someone with OCPD is slow, difficult, and rare.

Adjusting your expectations means accepting the reality of who your partner is, rather than holding onto the hope that they will become someone they are not. It means focusing on what you can control—your own behavior, your boundaries, and your own well-being.

Understanding the OCPD mindset is the foundation for navigating this complex relationship. Now that we have clarified this distinction, we can look more closely at the specific behaviors that characterize the OCPD spouse.

Understanding the Core Differences

- OCD is an anxiety disorder driven by irrational fears; OCPD is a personality disorder driven by rigid values and beliefs.

- OCD symptoms are *ego-dystonic* (unwanted and distressing). The person knows their behaviors are irrational.

- OCPD symptoms are *ego-syntonic* (consistent with the person's self-concept). The person believes their behaviors are correct and desirable.

- The ego-syntonic nature of OCPD makes it difficult for the individual to recognize they have a problem, leading them to blame others for conflicts.

- People with OCPD rarely seek help on their own because they do not believe they need to change.

Chapter 3: The Hallmarks of the OCPD Spouse

When you live with someone with OCPD, the disorder permeates every aspect of your life together. It's not just an occasional annoyance; it's a constant presence, shaping the atmosphere of your home and the dynamics of your relationship. While every individual with OCPD is different, there are common hallmark behaviors that emerge from the core traits of orderliness, perfectionism, and control.

Recognizing these hallmarks can be incredibly validating. It helps you connect the dots and see that the seemingly unrelated behaviors—the arguments about money, the long hours at work, the constant corrections—are actually all part of the same pattern. It helps you understand that you are not imagining things, and you are not overreacting.

In this chapter, we will explore the major hallmarks of the OCPD spouse.

The "One Right Way" Mentality and Moral Superiority

This is the cornerstone of the OCPD personality. The belief that there is a single, correct way to do everything, and that their way is it. This applies to everything from the mundane (how to stack the dishwasher) to the significant (how to raise children or manage finances).

This isn't just a preference; it's a conviction. They genuinely believe that their methods are superior, more efficient, more logical, and more ethical than any other approach.

The Tyranny of the Trivial

The "One Right Way" mentality often shows up most strongly in the small, everyday tasks. This is what makes living with an OCPD spouse so exhausting. Everything is a potential battleground.

- **Chores:** There is a specific way to fold the laundry or organize the refrigerator. If you do it differently, you will be corrected, criticized, or they will simply redo it after you.
- **Routines:** They often have rigid routines for mornings, evenings, weekends. These routines must be followed exactly, and any disruption can cause significant distress or anger.
- **Conversations:** They may correct your grammar, challenge the accuracy of your storytelling, or insist on precise definitions of words.

The focus on the "right way" often overshadows the purpose of the activity. The goal of doing laundry is to have clean clothes. But for the OCPD spouse, the goal is to do the laundry *correctly*.

The Illusion of Logic

The OCPD spouse often presents their way as the most logical and sensible approach. They will provide detailed explanations for why their method is superior. They genuinely believe their reasoning is objective and irrefutable.

If you try to argue with their logic, you will likely find yourself in a frustrating and unwinnable debate. They are skilled at intellectualizing their preferences and dismissing alternative viewpoints.

Moral Superiority: The Ethical High Ground

The "One Right Way" mentality often extends into the realm of morality and ethics. Individuals with OCPD tend to have a very rigid sense of right and wrong. They adhere strictly to rules and regulations and expect others to do the same.

This can manifest as being overly conscientious, scrupulous, and judgmental. They may be quick to criticize others for minor infractions.

In the marriage, this moral superiority can be suffocating. The OCPD spouse often assumes the role of the "responsible adult," while the partner is cast as the "irresponsible child."

They may criticize your choices, framing their perspective as the only ethical or moral choice. They struggle to agree to disagree, because they see disagreement as a moral failing.

This judgmental attitude creates emotional distance. You feel constantly scrutinized and found lacking. You may start hiding things from your partner to avoid their criticism, which further erodes trust and intimacy.

The Workaholic: Excessive Devotion to Productivity at the Expense of Connection

Excessive devotion to work and productivity is a hallmark of OCPD. This is not just about working long hours to earn money. It is a compulsion to be constantly productive, driven by a deep-seated belief that relaxation is wasteful and self-indulgent.

The Need to Be "Doing Something"

The OCPD spouse is often uncomfortable with downtime. They feel anxious or guilty when they are not engaged in a productive activity. Weekends and vacations are not for relaxation; they are opportunities to tackle projects or get ahead on work.

If you try to get them to relax, they may become irritable or dismissive. This constant need to be busy creates a frenetic atmosphere in the home. You may feel pressured to keep up with their pace or feel guilty for wanting to rest.

Work as a Sanctuary

The workplace often provides a sanctuary for the OCPD individual. It is a structured environment where their meticulousness and dedication are often rewarded. They may feel more comfortable and in control at work than they do at home.

They may prioritize work over family events, anniversaries, or holidays. They might routinely bring work home and spend evenings and weekends immersed in their job. Research has shown a strong link between OCPD and workaholism, often driven by their perfectionism and fear of making mistakes (Pinto et al., 2014).

The Emotional Impact on the Marriage

When you are married to a workaholic, you often feel lonely, neglected, and unimportant. You feel like you are second place to their job.

The excessive focus on productivity leaves little room for emotional connection and intimacy. Conversations are often transactional, focused on logistics and tasks rather than feelings and experiences.

If you try to address the imbalance, they may defend their work ethic as a virtue. They might say they are working hard for the family. They struggle to see the emotional cost of their behavior.

Frugality and Control: Stinginess with Money, Time, and Affection

Another common hallmark of the OCPD spouse is a miserly or stingy approach to resources. This is not just about being careful with money. It is about control and a deep-seated fear of scarcity.

Financial Control

The OCPD individual often hoards money for future catastrophes (American Psychiatric Association, 2022). They may be extremely frugal, even to the point of self-deprivation. They might resist spending money on things they deem unnecessary, even if they can afford it.

In the marriage, this frugality often manifests as financial control. The OCPD spouse may insist on managing the finances, monitoring the partner's spending, and imposing strict budgets.

They may criticize your purchases or make you feel guilty for spending money on yourself. This can create a significant power imbalance in the relationship, leaving you feeling dependent and resentful.

Consider the case of Sarah and Mark. Mark has OCPD. He insists on reviewing the grocery receipt every week, questioning Sarah about why she bought the name-brand cereal instead of the generic version. Although they have a substantial savings account, Mark constantly talks about the need to save more. Sarah feels suffocated by his financial control.

Stinginess with Time

The stinginess also extends to time. The OCPD spouse is often rigid about schedules and reluctant to deviate from their routine. They may view time as a commodity that must be maximized for productivity.

They may try to control how you spend your time as well, criticizing you for "wasting time" or being inefficient. They may be inflexible about plans, becoming agitated if you are late or if things don't go according to schedule.

Emotional Stinginess

Perhaps the most painful aspect of this stinginess is the lack of emotional generosity. Individuals with OCPD often struggle to express warmth, affection, and empathy. They may view emotions as messy and unpredictable.

They may be emotionally reserved or distant. They may struggle to say "I love you," offer compliments, or provide comfort when you are distressed.

This emotional stinginess creates a deep sense of loneliness and disconnection in the marriage. You feel starved for affection and validation. The OCPD spouse may express their love through acts of service, like working hard, but their inability to express emotional warmth can leave their partner feeling empty.

The Inability to Delegate or Trust Others

The final hallmark of the OCPD spouse is a profound inability to delegate tasks or trust others to do things correctly. This stems from their perfectionism and their belief in the "One Right Way."

Micromanagement and Hovering

If the OCPD spouse does ask you to do something, they will likely provide excessively detailed instructions and then hover over you while you do it. They are constantly checking your work, offering "helpful" suggestions, or correcting your mistakes.

This micromanagement is infuriating. It makes you feel untrusted and incompetent. You may feel like an employee rather than a partner.

Redoing Tasks

Often, the OCPD spouse will simply redo the task themselves after you have completed it. They might re-wash the dishes or re-fold the laundry.

This behavior is deeply invalidating. It sends the message that your efforts are not good enough and that they do not value your contribution.

The Burden of Responsibility

Because they cannot delegate, the OCPD spouse often takes on an excessive amount of responsibility. They try to do everything themselves.

This can lead to burnout, stress, and resentment. They may complain about how much they have to do, but they refuse to accept help. They may adopt a martyr complex, feeling overburdened and unappreciated.

The Impact on Teamwork

The inability to delegate destroys teamwork in the marriage. A healthy marriage is a partnership. In an OCPD marriage, the relationship is often hierarchical, with the OCPD spouse acting as the manager and the partner as the subordinate.

This lack of trust extends beyond household tasks. The OCPD spouse may not trust your judgment or your ability to handle situations on your own. They may constantly second-guess you or try to control your behavior.

Recognizing these hallmarks is crucial for understanding the dynamics of your marriage. These behaviors are part of a pervasive pattern of rigidity and control.

By identifying these patterns, you can begin to see how they affect you. You can start to separate the behavior from your own self-worth and recognize that their criticism and control are symptoms of their disorder, not a reflection of your competence or value.

Identifying the Hallmarks

- The OCPD spouse often exhibits a "one right way" mentality, believing their methods are superior and leading to a sense of moral superiority.

- Workaholism is common, driven by a need for productivity, often at the expense of the relationship.

- Frugality and control often manifest as stinginess with money, time, and affection, leading to emotional distance and conflict.

- The inability to delegate leads to micromanagement, eroding the partner's self-esteem.

- Recognizing these patterns is the first step toward understanding the relationship dynamic and developing coping strategies.

Chapter 4: What Drives the Control? The Hidden Anxiety

Living with an OCPD partner can feel like living with a dictator. Their need for control is so pervasive, their rules so rigid, that it can be easy to view them as simply stubborn, mean, or power-hungry. You see the outward behavior—the criticism, the demands, the emotional distance—and it's hard to imagine what could possibly justify it.

But if we want to understand the OCPD personality, we have to look beneath the surface. We have to ask the question: What drives the control?

The answer, surprisingly, is often **anxiety**.

The OCPD individual may not appear anxious on the surface. They often seem calm, collected, and in charge. But beneath the veneer of perfectionism and control lies a deep-seated fear of chaos, uncertainty, and error.

Their rigid behaviors are not actually about power, at least not primarily. They are defense mechanisms designed to manage this underlying anxiety and create a sense of safety in a world that feels unpredictable and threatening.

Understanding this hidden anxiety is crucial. It doesn't excuse their behavior, but it does help explain it. It can help you depersonalize their criticism and develop more effective strategies for coping with their rigidity.

Exploring the Roots of OCPD (Genetics, Upbringing)

Where does this deep-seated anxiety and the resulting rigid personality structure come from? It is likely a combination of genetic predisposition and environmental factors.

The Role of Genetics and Temperament

Some people are simply born with a temperament that makes them more prone to anxiety, rigidity, and perfectionism. They may be more sensitive to stress and more inclined toward order and structure.

Research suggests that OCPD has a genetic component. If a person has a family history of OCPD or other anxiety disorders, they may be at higher risk (Torgersen et al., 2000). Genetics alone do not determine destiny, but they can create a vulnerability.

The Impact of Upbringing and Early Experiences

The environment in which a person grows up plays a significant role in shaping their personality. Certain types of upbringing are more likely to contribute to the development of OCPD.

1. Rigid and Controlling Parenting:

Children raised in environments where rules are rigid, expectations are high, and mistakes are punished severely may learn that the only way to be safe and accepted is to be perfect and in control.

They may internalize the belief that any deviation from the rules will lead to catastrophe. They may develop a harsh inner critic that constantly monitors their behavior.

2. Emotionally Unavailable or Unpredictable Parenting:

Children raised by parents who are emotionally unavailable or unpredictable may turn to control and order as a way to manage their anxiety and create a sense of stability.

If they cannot rely on their caregivers for comfort, they may learn to rely on themselves and their own rigid rules. They may become hyper-independent and distrustful of others.

3. Conditional Love and Approval:

Children who receive love only when they meet their parents' high standards may learn that their worth is dependent on their performance. They may develop a deep-seated fear of failure and rejection.

They may strive for perfectionism as a way to earn love and avoid criticism. They may learn to suppress their emotions and focus on productivity and achievement.

These early experiences can help us understand how the rigid patterns of thinking and behavior develop.

Understanding That Control Is a Defense Mechanism Against Deep-Seated Anxiety and Fear of Chaos

In the OCPD mind, the world is a dangerous and unpredictable place. Chaos lurks around every corner. Mistakes lead to disaster. Uncertainty is intolerable.

To manage this overwhelming anxiety, the OCPD individual develops a system of rigid rules and procedures. This system creates an illusion of control and predictability. It provides a sense of safety and security.

The Function of Rigidity

The rigidity you see in your OCPD partner is not just a preference for order. It is a defense mechanism designed to ward off the fear of the unknown.

- **Rules and Lists:** Create a sense of structure and predictability.
- **Perfectionism:** Is an attempt to avoid criticism and failure. If they can do everything perfectly, they believe they can protect themselves from harm.
- **Workaholism:** Provides a distraction from uncomfortable emotions and a sense of control.
- **Frugality:** Is an attempt to prepare for future catastrophes.

When you challenge their rules or try to introduce flexibility, you are not just challenging their preferences. You are threatening their defense system. You are exposing them to the anxiety they are desperately trying to avoid.

The Fear of Error

At the core of OCPD is a profound fear of making mistakes. They believe that any error, no matter how small, will have catastrophic consequences.

This fear drives their perfectionism and their need to control every detail. They check and recheck their work. This fear of error also drives their criticism of you. When you make a mistake, it triggers their anxiety. They feel compelled to correct you to prevent disaster and restore order.

The Fear of Emotions

Individuals with OCPD are often deeply uncomfortable with emotions. Emotions are messy, unpredictable, and illogical. They cannot be controlled.

They may try to suppress their own emotions, particularly vulnerable feelings like sadness, fear, and shame. They may also be dismissive of your emotions, viewing them as irrational or excessive.

This emotional avoidance is another defense mechanism. It protects them from the discomfort of vulnerability and the fear of losing control.

The Cycle of Anxiety and Control

The tragedy of OCPD is that the defense mechanisms designed to manage anxiety often end up creating more anxiety.

The relentless pursuit of perfection leads to stress and burnout. The need for control damages relationships, leading to isolation and conflict. The avoidance of emotions prevents them from experiencing the joy and connection that make life meaningful. They are trapped in a cycle, constantly striving for a sense of safety that remains elusive.

Cognitive Distortions: Black-and-White Thinking and Catastrophizing

The anxiety that drives OCPD is fueled by specific patterns of distorted thinking, known as cognitive distortions. These are habitual ways of thinking that are biased and inaccurate.

1. Black-and-White Thinking (Dichotomous Thinking)

This is the tendency to see things in extremes, with no middle ground. Things are either right or wrong, good or bad, perfect or ruined.

This black-and-white thinking underlies the "One Right Way" mentality. If their way is right, then any other way must be wrong. There is no room for nuance or compromise.

In the marriage, this manifests as:

- **Impossible Standards:** If something is not done perfectly, it is considered a failure.
- **Judgmental Attitude:** People are either responsible or irresponsible.
- **Inability to Compromise:** Compromise is seen as sacrificing principles.

They genuinely cannot see the gray areas.

2. Catastrophizing

This is the tendency to assume the worst possible outcome will happen. Minor problems are blown out of proportion and viewed as disasters.

This cognitive distortion drives the fear of error. The OCPD individual believes that any mistake will lead to catastrophe.

- If they are late for an appointment, they believe their reputation will be ruined.
- If they forget to pay a bill, they believe their electricity will be cut off.

This catastrophizing justifies their rigid adherence to rules. They are constantly trying to prevent the disaster they believe is imminent.

3. "Should" Statements

This is the belief that things *should* be a certain way. OCPD individuals have a rigid set of rules about how they and others should behave.

- "I should always be productive."
- "People should always be on time."

When these "should" statements are violated, they experience frustration and anger. They believe the world should conform to their rules.

4. Emotional Reasoning

This is the belief that if you feel something, it must be true. The OCPD individual often mistakes their anxiety for a sign that something is actually wrong.

If they feel anxious about a decision, they believe the decision must be wrong. This emotional reasoning reinforces their rigidity. They trust their gut feelings over objective evidence, even when those feelings are driven by distorted thinking.

How Recognizing the Anxiety Can Foster Empathy (Without Excusing the Behavior)

When you are on the receiving end of control, it can be difficult to feel empathy for your OCPD partner. You feel hurt and angry, and rightfully so.

However, recognizing the anxiety beneath the control can help you shift your perspective.

Depersonalizing the Criticism

When your partner criticizes you for loading the dishwasher "wrong," it feels like a personal attack.

But if you understand that their criticism is driven by their anxiety about disorder, you can start to depersonalize it. It's not about you. It's about their need for control to manage their own internal discomfort.

Shifting from Anger to Pity (Sometimes)

When you see the rigidity not as a choice, but as a defense mechanism, you might find yourself feeling a sense of pity for your partner. You see how trapped they are by their own rules, how much joy they miss out on because of their fear of imperfection.

This shift can help reduce the intensity of your own emotional reactions.

The Crucial Caveat: Empathy Does Not Mean Excusing

Here is the most important point of this chapter: **Understanding the cause of their behavior does not excuse the behavior.**

Just because your partner is driven by anxiety does not mean you have to accept being treated poorly. You have the right to be treated with respect. You have the right to set boundaries and protect your own well-being.

Empathy is not about letting them off the hook. It is about understanding their limitations and motivations so you can make informed decisions about how to proceed.

It is possible to hold both empathy for their struggle and accountability for their actions.

You can say, "I understand that you feel anxious when things are not done a certain way. But it is not okay for you to criticize me and treat me with disrespect."

Focusing on What You Can Control

Recognizing the deep-seated nature of their anxiety also helps you accept the limits of your own influence. You cannot "fix" their anxiety or change their personality structure. You cannot argue them out of their distorted thinking.

What you can do is focus on what you can control: your reactions, your boundaries, and your choices.

By understanding the hidden drivers of their behavior, you can stop engaging in unproductive arguments and start developing strategies that protect your own mental health and create space for positive change in the relationship.

Understanding the Drivers

- The rigid control and perfectionism of OCPD are often driven by deep-seated anxiety and a fear of chaos, uncertainty, and error.
- Control is a defense mechanism designed to create a sense of safety and predictability in a world that feels threatening.
- Cognitive distortions, such as black-and-white thinking, catastrophizing, and "should" statements, fuel the anxiety and justify the rigid behaviors.
- Recognizing the anxiety beneath the control can help you depersonalize the criticism and foster empathy.
- Empathy does not mean excusing the behavior. You have the right to set boundaries and demand respectful treatment.

- Understanding the drivers of OCPD helps you accept the limits of your influence and focus on what you can control.

Chapter 5: Walking on Eggshells: The Emotional Toll

When you first realize your partner might have OCPD, the focus is usually on *their* behavior. Their rigidity, their rules, their need for control. It's all very loud, very present in the relationship. But what about you? What happens to the person living in the shadow of that rigidity?

The impact is often slow and insidious. It's not usually one big dramatic event. It's a gradual erosion, like water dripping on a stone, slowly wearing away your sense of self, your confidence, and your peace of mind.

People living with OCPD partners often use the same phrase: "I feel like I'm walking on eggshells." This means you are constantly hyper-vigilant. You are always monitoring your behavior, anticipating their reactions, and trying to avoid triggering their criticism or anger. You are tiptoeing around their rules, trying not to make a sound, trying not to disturb the fragile peace.

Living in this state of constant tension takes a significant emotional toll. It's exhausting. And it changes you. In this chapter, we are going to look closely at the ways that living with an OCPD partner affects your mental and emotional health. It's important to recognize these changes in yourself so you can begin to address them.

The Impact of Constant Criticism and Correction

Let's start with the most pervasive aspect of living with an OCPD partner: the constant stream of criticism and correction.

As we discussed earlier, the OCPD individual believes there is "One Right Way" to do everything. And they feel compelled to point out when you deviate from that way. This isn't just occasional feedback. It's a running commentary on your life.

The "Helpful" Correction That Isn't Helpful

The criticism often comes disguised as "help." They aren't criticizing you, they insist; they are just showing you a better, more efficient way.

- "You shouldn't chop the vegetables like that. It's more efficient this way."
- "You missed a spot while vacuuming. Here, let me show you."
- "Why did you take that route? The other way is faster by two minutes."

These comments might seem minor in isolation. You might even tell yourself you're being too sensitive. But when they happen day after day, year after year, they accumulate. It's like death by a thousand cuts. They create a pervasive sense that you are constantly being evaluated and found lacking.

The OCPD partner genuinely believes they are being helpful. They don't understand why you would be upset by their suggestions. In their mind, they are simply sharing objective facts about the best way to operate. But the impact on you is profound. You feel micromanaged, scrutinized, and disrespected. It feels like you are constantly under a microscope.

The Moral Judgment

The criticism often carries a heavy moral weight. It's not just that you did something inefficiently; it's that you are lazy, irresponsible, or careless.

The OCPD partner's rigid adherence to rules means they often view deviations from their standards as moral failings. If you want to relax on a Saturday instead of being productive, you are self-indulgent. If you don't rinse your plate before putting it in the dishwasher, you are inconsiderate.

This moral judgment is incredibly painful because it strikes at the core of your character. You start to feel ashamed of yourself, even when you have done nothing inherently wrong. You are simply being human in a relationship that demands perfection.

The Death of Spontaneity

The constant criticism also kills spontaneity. You become afraid to try new things or express yourself freely because you know you will be judged.

Think about it. Why start a new hobby if you know your efforts will be critiqued before you even begin? Why cook a new recipe if you know your technique will be corrected at every step?

Life becomes constricted. You shrink yourself to fit into the narrow space allowed by their rules. You stop initiating activities. You stop sharing opinions. You simply try to blend into the background.

Case Example: The Dishwasher Dilemma

Jenna used to enjoy cooking. But her husband, Michael, who has OCPD, constantly monitored her in the kitchen. He would correct her technique and complain about the mess she made. When she finished cooking, Michael would reorganize the dishwasher, explaining that her method was inefficient because it didn't maximize the space.

Jenna started to dread being in the kitchen. She felt anxious and incompetent every time she tried to prepare a meal. She stopped cooking elaborate meals and relied on frozen dinners. When Michael complained about the quality of the food, Jenna felt a surge of resentment. The constant criticism had eroded her enjoyment and her confidence, turning a simple daily activity into a source of intense stress.

The Erosion of Self-Esteem and Decision-Making Confidence

When you are constantly told that you are wrong, incompetent, or inadequate, you start to believe it. It's a simple psychological reality.

The erosion of self-esteem is one of the most damaging consequences of living with an OCPD partner.

Second-Guessing Yourself

It starts with internalizing their critical voice. You hear their corrections even when they are not physically present. You might be getting dressed and think, "He would say this outfit doesn't match." You might be writing an email at work and think, "I need to check this three more times for errors."

You start to second-guess every decision you make, big or small. You lose trust in your own judgment. The confident person you once were begins to fade away.

Analysis Paralysis

This constant second-guessing can lead to what we call *analysis paralysis*. You become so afraid of making the "wrong" decision—because you know the consequences will be a lecture or a sigh of disapproval—that you become unable to make any decision at all.

You might agonize over simple choices, like what to buy at the grocery store. You try to anticipate their preferences and avoid their criticism. Your own preferences? They get lost in the process. You stop knowing what you actually want because your focus is entirely on what they demand.

The Loss of Identity

Over time, this erosion of confidence can lead to a profound loss of identity. You become so focused on meeting their standards and avoiding their disapproval that you forget who you are and what you want.

You may give up hobbies, friendships, and interests that they criticize or deem "unproductive." You may even adopt their opinions and values, even if they contradict your own, simply because it's easier than fighting.

This loss of self is devastating. You may wake up one day and realize you don't recognize yourself anymore. You feel empty, lost, and disconnected from your own life. You are living their life, according to their rules, and you are merely a supporting character in their script.

The "Freeze" Response: Shutting Down to Avoid Conflict

When we are faced with a threat, our nervous system activates the stress response, commonly known as fight, flight, or freeze. This is an ancient survival mechanism designed to keep us safe.

In a relationship with an OCPD partner, you are constantly faced with the threat of criticism, judgment, and conflict. Your nervous system perceives this emotional environment as dangerous. But the usual responses often don't work.

- **Fight:** If you try to fight back, you often find yourself in an unwinnable battle. The OCPD partner will out-argue you, exhaust you, and make you feel irrational or overly emotional. Fighting rarely leads to resolution; it usually just leads to escalation.
- **Flight:** If you try to flee, you may feel trapped by financial constraints, family obligations, or guilt. And even if you walk away from a specific argument, you still live in the same house. The threat remains.

When fight and flight are not viable options, the nervous system often resorts to the **freeze** response.

Shutting Down Emotionally

The freeze response involves shutting down emotionally and behaviorally to minimize the threat. It's like an animal playing dead. You become numb, detached, and compliant.

You might find yourself automatically agreeing with your partner, even when you strongly disagree. You might apologize for things you didn't do wrong just to restore peace. You hide your true feelings. You just want the interaction to be over.

This shutting down is a survival mechanism. But it comes at a significant cost. When you shut down emotionally, you lose access to your own feelings, needs, and desires. You are surviving, but you are not thriving.

The Fawn Response: Appeasing the Threat

A related response, often discussed in the context of complex trauma, is the *fawn* response. This involves immediately trying to please and placate the other person to avoid conflict (Walker, 2013). It's characterized by excessive people-pleasing and prioritizing the needs of others above your own.

In an OCPD marriage, the fawn response is often strongly reinforced. When you comply with their demands, you are rewarded with temporary peace. When you assert yourself, you are punished with criticism, anger, or the silent treatment.

You learn very quickly that the safest way to exist in the relationship is to be compliant. You anticipate their needs. You apologize preemptively. But this means sacrificing your own autonomy. You are essentially erasing yourself to maintain the relationship.

The Long-Term Impact

While these responses may help you survive in the short term, they are damaging in the long term. They reinforce the power imbalance and perpetuate the cycle of control and submission.

They also prevent you from addressing the underlying issues. When you shut down or placate, you are not communicating your needs or setting boundaries. You are signaling that the status quo is acceptable, even when it is destroying you from the inside out.

Recognizing Signs of Anxiety, Depression, and Burnout in Yourself

Living in a state of constant tension and emotional deprivation takes a heavy toll on your mental health. Partners of OCPD individuals are at high risk for anxiety, depression, and burnout.

It's crucial to recognize the signs of these conditions in yourself.

Anxiety and Hypervigilance

Anxiety is characterized by excessive worry, fear, and tension. In an OCPD marriage, anxiety often manifests as *hypervigilance*.

You are constantly on edge, scanning the environment for potential threats. You might feel restless, irritable, and unable to relax. When you hear their car in the driveway, your heart starts pounding. You may have difficulty sleeping or concentrating because your mind is racing with "what if" scenarios.

The constant stress of walking on eggshells keeps your nervous system in a state of high alert, and it never gets a chance to reset.

Depression and Hopelessness

Depression is characterized by persistent sadness, loss of interest in activities you once enjoyed, and feelings of worthlessness and hopelessness.

In an OCPD marriage, depression often stems from the erosion of self-esteem, the lack of emotional connection, and the feeling of being trapped. You try and try, but nothing changes.

The constant criticism and lack of positive reinforcement can lead to a deep sense of hopelessness. You may feel like nothing you do will ever be good enough, and that the relationship will never improve. This hopelessness is a hallmark of depression.

Burnout and Exhaustion

Burnout is a state of emotional, physical, and mental exhaustion caused by prolonged and excessive stress. It is characterized by feelings of cynicism, detachment, and a sense of ineffectiveness (Maslach & Jackson, 1981).

In an OCPD marriage, burnout often results from the relentless demands of trying to meet impossible standards, the emotional labor of managing your partner's rigidity, and the lack of support and appreciation. You are constantly giving, and receiving very little in return.

Recognizing the Connection

It's crucial to recognize that these symptoms—the anxiety, the depression, the burnout—are not a sign of weakness or failure on your part. They are a normal response to an abnormal situation.

Living with an OCPD partner is inherently stressful and damaging. Your emotional toll is a direct consequence of the relationship dynamics.

Acknowledging this reality is the first step toward healing. It allows you to stop blaming yourself and start focusing on protecting your own well-being.

In the next chapter, we will explore another dimension of the emotional toll: the profound loneliness and lack of intimacy that characterize many OCPD marriages.

The Impact on You

- Living with an OCPD partner often leads to a state of hypervigilance, described as "walking on eggshells."

- Constant criticism and correction erode your self-esteem and decision-making confidence over time. This is sometimes called "death by a thousand cuts."

- You may internalize their critical voice, leading to second-guessing, analysis paralysis, and eventually a loss of your own identity.

- The "freeze" response (shutting down emotionally) and the "fawn" response (excessive people-pleasing) are common survival mechanisms used to avoid conflict, but they require sacrificing your autonomy.

- Partners of OCPD individuals are at high risk for anxiety, depression, and burnout. Recognizing these symptoms as a response to the relationship dynamics, rather than a personal failing, is the first step toward healing.

Chapter 6: The Loneliest Marriage

Emotional Distance and Intimacy

There is a particular kind of loneliness that comes from being in a relationship with someone who is physically present but emotionally absent. This is the reality for many people married to an OCPD partner.

On the surface, the marriage might look perfect. The house is clean, the bills are paid on time, the schedule is organized. But beneath the surface, there is a profound emotional void.

The very traits that define OCPD—the preoccupation with order, the need for control, the rigid adherence to rules—create a barrier to emotional connection and intimacy. Relationships require flexibility, vulnerability, and empathy. These are qualities that the OCPD individual often struggles with profoundly.

The result is a marriage that feels transactional rather than relational. It's focused on tasks and performance rather than feelings and connection. It's what many describe as the loneliest marriage.

Why OCPD Individuals Struggle with Expressing Warmth and Vulnerability

To understand the emotional distance in an OCPD marriage, we have to understand the OCPD relationship with emotions. It's complicated, to say the least.

Emotions as Chaos

As we discussed previously, the OCPD individual is driven by a deep-seated anxiety about chaos and uncertainty. Emotions, by their very nature, are messy, unpredictable, and illogical. They cannot be easily categorized, scheduled, or controlled.

For the OCPD person, emotions are a threat to their sense of order and stability. They may try to suppress their own feelings, particularly vulnerable emotions like sadness, fear, or shame. They may view emotional expression—especially strong displays of emotion—as a sign of weakness, irrationality, or being "out of control."

The Focus on Logic and Intellect

The OCPD individual prefers to operate in the realm of logic and intellect. They struggle with the subjective, messy world of feelings.

When you try to express your emotions, they may respond with logic and analysis rather than empathy and comfort. If you say, "I feel sad," they might try to "fix" your sadness by offering solutions or, more likely, dismissing your feelings as illogical. "You have no reason to be sad," they might say. Or, "Being sad isn't going to solve the problem."

This intellectualization of emotions is incredibly invalidating. It makes you feel misunderstood, dismissed, and fundamentally alone with your feelings. You learn quickly that your partner is not a safe person to turn to for emotional support.

Alexithymia: The Difficulty Naming Feelings

Some individuals with OCPD also experience *alexithymia*, which is a clinical term for difficulty identifying and describing emotions. They may genuinely not know how they feel. They might experience physical symptoms—like tension or fatigue—but they struggle to connect these symptoms to an underlying emotion. They lack the vocabulary to express their inner world.

This difficulty with emotional awareness significantly contributes to the emotional distance. If they cannot understand their own feelings, they certainly cannot understand or empathize with yours.

The Fear of Vulnerability

Intimacy requires vulnerability. It requires letting your guard down and exposing your authentic self, flaws and all.

For the OCPD individual, vulnerability is terrifying. It means relinquishing control and opening themselves up to the possibility of criticism or rejection. Their entire personality is structured around achieving perfection to avoid criticism. Being vulnerable means admitting they are not perfect.

They may hide behind a facade of competence and self-sufficiency. They may resist expressing affection or dependence on you because needing someone else feels weak. This fear of vulnerability creates an impenetrable wall between you and your partner. You cannot connect with someone who refuses to be seen.

The Lack of Warmth and Affection

The result of this discomfort with emotions is a marked lack of warmth and affection in the relationship. The OCPD individual often struggles to express positive emotions, such as love, joy, or appreciation.

They may rarely offer compliments or words of affirmation. They might find it difficult to say "I love you." They may be uncomfortable with physical affection, such as hugging, cuddling, or holding hands.

They often express their love through acts of service—working hard, providing financial security, maintaining the household. And they expect these practical expressions of care to be enough. They may become defensive if you ask for more emotional connection, pointing to all the things they *do* for you as proof of their love.

But these practical acts cannot replace the fundamental human need for emotional connection and warmth. The lack of affection leaves you feeling starved for love and validation.

Intimacy (Sexual and Emotional) Being Scheduled, Conditional, or Absent

The rigidity and control that characterize OCPD extend into the realm of intimacy, both emotional and sexual.

Emotional Intimacy: The Missing Connection

Emotional intimacy is the feeling of closeness that comes from sharing your innermost thoughts and feelings. In an OCPD marriage, this is often severely lacking. The OCPD partner's criticism, judgmental attitude, and emotional unavailability create an environment where it feels profoundly unsafe to be vulnerable.

Conversations are often superficial, focused on logistics, tasks, or intellectual debates. There is little room for the soft, vulnerable sharing that builds true connection.

Sexual Intimacy: The Chore of Sex

Sexual intimacy is also often strained. The OCPD partner's rigidity, perfectionism, and emotional distance can interfere significantly with sexual desire and satisfaction.

1. Scheduled Sex and Rigidity:

The OCPD individual often approaches sex with the same rigidity and planning as they approach everything else. Sex may become a scheduled activity, slotted into a specific time and day. This scheduling kills spontaneity and passion. Sex becomes another chore on the to-do list. The act itself might also be rigid, following a predictable routine with little room for variation.

2. Performance Anxiety and Criticism:

Their perfectionism can lead to performance anxiety in the bedroom. They may be overly focused on the mechanics of sex rather than the emotional experience. Furthermore, their critical nature may extend to the bedroom. They may criticize your appearance, your responses, or your performance. This makes it impossible to relax and enjoy the experience.

3. Conditional Sex:

In some OCPD marriages, sex becomes conditional. The OCPD partner may withhold sex as a way to punish you for perceived transgressions or reward you for compliance. Affection is only given when you have met their standards. This use of sex as a tool for control is damaging to the relationship and your self-esteem.

4. Absent Sex:

In many cases, sexual intimacy disappears altogether. The OCPD partner may have low sexual desire due to their preoccupation with work or their emotional detachment. They may view sex as messy, unpredictable, or simply a low priority. The lack of physical intimacy further exacerbates the emotional distance, leaving you feeling rejected and undesirable.

Case Example: The Transactional Marriage

Lisa and Tom have been married for 15 years. Tom has OCPD. Their life is highly structured. Tom works long hours and spends his weekends catching up on chores and projects.

Lisa feels desperately lonely. Tom rarely expresses affection. When she tries to talk to him about her feelings, he dismisses her as "overly emotional" and tells her she needs to be more resilient. Sex happens infrequently and feels mechanical.

Lisa feels like she is living with a business partner rather than a husband. She craves emotional connection and intimacy, but Tom seems incapable of providing it. The marriage is stable on the surface, but emotionally barren underneath.

Feeling Like an Employee or a Child Rather Than a Partner

One of the most painful aspects of the OCPD marriage is the erosion of the partnership dynamic. A healthy marriage is a relationship between equals. In an OCPD marriage, the relationship often becomes hierarchical. The OCPD partner's need for control and their belief in their own superiority create a dynamic where the partner feels like an employee or a child.

The Employee Role: Micromanaged and Evaluated

You may feel like an employee working for an incredibly demanding boss. The OCPD partner assigns tasks, provides excessively detailed instructions, and evaluates your performance against their rigid standards.

They micromanage your behavior, constantly checking your work and correcting your mistakes. This dynamic is exhausting and demoralizing. You feel untrusted and incompetent. You are constantly undergoing a performance review, and the feedback is always "needs improvement."

The Child Role: Controlled and Disciplined

You may also feel like a child being raised by a strict, unforgiving parent. The OCPD partner sets the rules, monitors your behavior, and disciplines you (through criticism, lectures, or the silent treatment) when you step out of line.

They may control your spending, dictate your schedule, and criticize your choices. They may treat you as irresponsible or incapable of making your own decisions. This dynamic is infantilizing and disempowering. You feel suffocated and controlled.

The Lack of Partnership

In both dynamics, what is missing is the sense of partnership. You do not feel like you are part of a team. You feel like you are working for or living under the rule of your partner. This lack of partnership creates a deep sense of resentment and loneliness. You long for a relationship where you feel respected and valued as an equal.

Grieving the Loss of Spontaneous Connection

Living with an OCPD partner often involves a process of grieving. You grieve the loss of the relationship you thought you would have. And you grieve the loss of the spontaneous connection that makes life joyful and meaningful.

The Death of Spontaneity

Spontaneity is the lifeblood of a healthy relationship. It's the impromptu date night, the unexpected compliment, the shared laughter over a silly mistake.

In an OCPD marriage, spontaneity is often viewed as a threat. It disrupts the order and control that the OCPD partner craves. Life becomes rigid and predictable. Everything is planned, scheduled, and controlled. There is little room for surprise or delight.

You might try to introduce spontaneity, but your efforts are often met with resistance or criticism. Your partner might complain that you are being impulsive or irresponsible. Over time, you stop trying.

The Grief of Unmet Needs

The grief in an OCPD marriage is often complicated by the fact that the relationship is ongoing. You are grieving the loss of something you never fully had, but that you desperately long for.

You grieve the unmet need for emotional intimacy, for physical affection, for validation and acceptance.

This grief is often invisible to the outside world. People see the façade of your marriage, but they do not see the emptiness within.

Acknowledging the loneliness of the OCPD marriage is a crucial step toward healing. It is important to validate your own experience and recognize that your needs for emotional connection and intimacy are legitimate and important.

In the next chapter, we will explore the specific tactics that the OCPD partner uses to maintain control and dominance in the relationship.

The Emotional Void

- The OCPD marriage is often characterized by profound emotional distance and loneliness, despite the appearance of stability.

- OCPD individuals struggle with expressing warmth and vulnerability because they view emotions as messy and unpredictable, prioritizing logic over feeling.
- They may experience alexithymia (difficulty identifying emotions) and often struggle with empathy.
- Intimacy, both sexual and emotional, is often scheduled, conditional, or absent, leading to frustration and disconnection.
- The hierarchical dynamic often leaves the partner feeling like an employee or a child rather than an equal partner.
- Grieving the loss of spontaneous connection and the unmet need for intimacy is a common experience for partners of OCPD individuals.

Chapter 7: Recognizing Control and Manipulation Tactics

In a marriage with an OCPD individual, the dynamic is often skewed. The OCPD partner's need for perfection and order drives a deeper need for interpersonal control. They need things to be done their way, not just because they prefer it, but because it alleviates their anxiety and validates their worldview.

This need for control often manifests in various tactics—some overt, some subtle—that aim to maintain dominance and ensure compliance. It's important to understand that these tactics may not always be conscious or malicious. Often, the OCPD individual genuinely believes they are acting in the best interest of the family. They see their control as necessary to prevent chaos.

But regardless of the intention, the impact on you is the same. You feel manipulated, silenced, and powerless. Recognizing these tactics is the first step to countering them. When you can name the behavior, you can begin to see the pattern and develop strategies to protect yourself.

The Subtle (and Not-so-Subtle) Ways OCPD Partners Maintain Dominance

Control in an OCPD marriage is often disguised as helpfulness, logic, or responsibility.

The Tyranny of Logic (Intellectual Bullying)

One of the most common ways OCPD partners maintain dominance is by insisting that their perspective is the only logical and rational one. They use their intellect and verbal skills to out-argue you and dismiss your viewpoint. This is sometimes referred to as intellectual bullying.

They may present their opinions as objective facts and their personal preferences as logical necessities. They will debate endlessly, using complex arguments or relentless questioning to overwhelm you and shut down the conversation. They are masters of the "logic trap."

If you try to express a perspective based on feelings or intuition, they may accuse you of being illogical or overly emotional. This insistence on their version of logic invalidates your feelings and experiences.

Unilateral Decision-Making

The OCPD partner often assumes control over decision-making, both big and small. They may make decisions without consulting you, or they may dismiss your input if it contradicts their own preferences. Even if they ask for your opinion, it often feels like a formality; they have already decided the outcome.

They genuinely believe their judgment is superior. They may view collaboration as inefficient or messy. This leaves you feeling marginalized and voiceless, like you have no say in your own life.

Financial Control

Money is a common arena for control. The OCPD partner's inherent frugality and fear of future catastrophes often lead them to exert excessive control over finances.

They may insist on managing all the money, monitoring your spending with forensic detail, and imposing strict, often unrealistic, budgets. They may criticize your purchases or make you feel guilty for spending money on yourself, even for necessities.

In extreme cases, they may restrict your access to bank accounts or give you an allowance. This financial control creates a significant power imbalance, leaving you feeling dependent and infantilized.

Micromanagement and Correction

The constant micromanagement and correction also function as a powerful form of control. It sends the message that you are incompetent and untrustworthy. It keeps you in a subordinate position, constantly striving for their approval and anxious about making mistakes. By keeping you focused on the small details—the "correct" way to fold a towel—they prevent you from questioning the larger patterns of control.

Guilt-Tripping and the Martyr Complex

Guilt is a potent tool for manipulation. The OCPD individual is often skilled at inducing guilt in their partner to ensure compliance.

The Power of "Should"

The OCPD worldview is governed by "shoulds." They have rigid beliefs about how people should behave. When you violate these "shoulds," they often react with disappointment and disapproval.

They might say things like:

- "You should have known better."
- "If you really loved me, you would do this."
- "I thought I could count on you."

These statements imply that you are morally failing them.

The Martyr Complex: The Burden of Responsibility

The OCPD individual often takes on an excessive amount of responsibility because they cannot delegate or trust others. This leads to a martyr complex. They feel overburdened, unappreciated, and resentful.

They often use their martyrdom to manipulate their partner. They might complain about how hard they work, how much they sacrifice, and how little help they receive.

They might say things like:

- "I have to do everything myself."

- "No one appreciates how much I do for this family."
- "I guess I'll just stay up late and finish this, since no one else will."

These statements are designed to make you feel guilty for their suffering and to compel you to comply with their demands. They use their self-sacrifice as leverage to maintain control.

Case Example: The Weekend Sacrifice

Jenna wanted to visit her sister for the weekend. Her husband, Tom (who has OCPD), didn't want her to go because it would disrupt his routine. Instead of saying this directly, Tom sighed heavily and said, "Well, I guess I'll just have to cancel my plans to organize the garage. I was really counting on this weekend to get that done. It's fine. I'll manage. I always do."

Tom's martyrdom induced guilt in Jenna. She felt selfish for wanting to see her sister. She canceled her trip. Tom maintained control over the weekend by leveraging Jenna's guilt.

Gaslighting: "You're Too Sensitive," "That's Inefficient," "I Never Said That."

Gaslighting is a form of psychological manipulation in which a person seeks to sow seeds of doubt in an individual, making them question their own memory, perception, or sanity (Sarkis, 2018).

In an OCPD marriage, gaslighting is often subtle and insidious. It stems from the OCPD individual's belief that their perspective is the only correct one. They genuinely cannot understand why you see things differently, so they assume your perception must be flawed.

Dismissing Your Reality

The most common form of gaslighting in an OCPD marriage is the dismissal of your feelings and experiences.

If you express hurt or frustration, they might say:

- "You're too sensitive."
- "You're overreacting."
- "That's not what happened."
- "I was just trying to help."

These statements invalidate your reality. They tell you that your feelings are wrong, that your perception is inaccurate. Over time, you start to doubt your own judgment. You start to believe that you are, in fact, too sensitive or irrational.

The Logic Trap in Gaslighting

The OCPD individual often uses logic as a weapon to undermine your perspective. They might analyze your feelings and explain why they are illogical or inefficient.

If you say, "I feel lonely when you work late every night," they might respond with a detailed explanation of why their work is necessary, implying that your loneliness is an irrational distraction from the more important goal of productivity. They use intellectualization to dismiss the validity of your emotional experience.

Denying or Distorting the Past

Another form of gaslighting is the denial or distortion of past events. If you confront them about something they said or did, they might flatly deny it ("I never said that") or distort the details to fit their narrative ("You misunderstood what I meant").

This can make you feel like you are losing your mind. You start to question your memory and your perception of reality. Gaslighting is a powerful tool for control because if you doubt your own reality, you are more likely to accept their reality.

The "Moving Goalpost" Phenomenon—Nothing Is Ever Good Enough

One of the most frustrating aspects of living with an OCPD partner is the experience of the "moving goalpost." You strive to meet their expectations, but as soon as you do, the expectations change. The target shifts. Nothing is ever good enough.

The Illusion of Perfection

The OCPD individual is driven by the pursuit of perfection. But perfection is an illusion. It is an unattainable goal. There is always something that can be improved, something that is flawed. This internal drive for perfection is projected onto you. They hold you to the same impossible standards that they hold themselves.

The Shifting Expectations

You might work hard to meet a specific demand. For example, your partner might complain that the house is messy. You spend the entire weekend cleaning and organizing.

You expect them to be pleased. But instead of praise, they point out the one thing you missed. "You did a good job, but you forgot to clean the baseboards."

Or they might change the standard. "The house is clean, but now we need to reorganize the closets."

The goalpost moves. The satisfaction remains elusive.

Case Example: The Never-Ending Project

David asked his wife, Maria, to help him landscape the backyard. He gave her detailed instructions on how to plant the flowers. Maria followed the instructions carefully.

When she finished, David inspected her work. He adjusted the position of several flowers, explaining that they were not perfectly aligned. Then he said, "Now we need to add mulch. But we need to make sure the mulch is spread evenly, exactly one inch deep."

Maria felt defeated. No matter how hard she tried, she could never meet David's standards.

The Impact of the Moving Goalpost

The moving goalpost phenomenon is demoralizing and exhausting. It creates a sense of hopelessness and learned helplessness. You start to believe that nothing you do will ever make a difference, so you stop trying. It also creates resentment. You feel like you are constantly striving for approval that is never given.

Recognizing these control and manipulation tactics is the first step toward reclaiming your power. When you can see the pattern, you can stop blaming yourself and start responding differently.

In the next chapter, we will explore what happens when the OCPD partner's control is challenged or threatened—the intense anger and rage that often erupts when their carefully constructed world begins to crumble.

Identifying the Tactics

- OCPD partners often maintain dominance through subtle tactics like intellectual bullying (the "logic trap"), unilateral decision-making, financial control, and micromanagement.
- Guilt-tripping and the martyr complex are common manipulation tactics used to induce guilt and ensure compliance.
- Gaslighting—the dismissal of your feelings and experiences—is a form of psychological manipulation that undermines your self-trust and connection to reality.
- The "moving goalpost" phenomenon—the constant shifting of expectations—creates a sense of hopelessness and ensures the partner can never feel "good enough."
- Recognizing these tactics is the first step toward reclaiming your power and protecting your well-being.

Chapter 8: When Control Crumbles: Anger Outbursts and Rage

For many people with OCPD, the outward presentation is one of control, logic, and emotional restraint. They often seem calm and collected. But beneath this controlled exterior lies a volcano of intense emotion that can erupt suddenly and unexpectedly.

This eruption of anger, often disproportionate to the situation, is one of the most confusing and frightening aspects of living with an OCPD partner. You might be having a seemingly normal conversation, and suddenly, you are faced with a barrage of rage, criticism, and accusation.

The anger is often triggered when their sense of control is threatened. When things don't go according to plan, when mistakes are made, or when their authority is challenged, their carefully constructed world begins to crumble. The anxiety that underlies their rigidity spikes, and it often surfaces as anger.

Understanding the OCPD Anger Cycle (Triggered by Loss of Control or Perceived Errors)

The OCPD anger cycle is predictable, once you understand the underlying mechanisms. It is not random. It is a direct response to a perceived threat to their internal order.

The Trigger: The Threat to Control

The trigger for the anger is often something that seems minor to you, but that represents a significant threat to the OCPD individual.

Common triggers include:

- **Mistakes and Errors:** When you make a mistake, even a small one, it confirms their fear that chaos is imminent.

- **Unpredictability and Change:** When plans change suddenly or routines are disrupted, it triggers their anxiety about the unknown.
- **Inefficiency and Waste:** When they perceive that time or resources are being wasted, it violates their core values.
- **Challenges to Authority:** When you question their judgment or assert your own autonomy, it threatens their sense of superiority and control.
- **Feeling Criticized:** Despite their critical nature, OCPD individuals are often hypersensitive to criticism themselves.

The Escalation: From Anxiety to Anger

When a trigger occurs, the OCPD individual experiences a rapid surge of anxiety. They feel overwhelmed and out of control.

But anxiety is a vulnerable emotion. It feels uncomfortable and weak. For the OCPD individual, who values strength and control, this vulnerability is intolerable.

So they convert the anxiety into anger. Anger is a powerful emotion. It feels strong and righteous. It allows them to externalize the threat and regain a sense of control. Anger is often considered a secondary emotion—a defense against the primary emotion of fear, sadness, or shame (Greenberg & Safran, 1987). In OCPD, the primary emotion is fear—the fear of chaos and error.

The Outburst: The Eruption of Rage

The outburst of anger can take many forms, from subtle irritation to explosive rage.

- **Criticism and Blame:** They may attack your character, question your competence, and blame you for the problem.
- **Lecturing and Moralizing:** They may launch into a long lecture about the "right way" to do things.

- **Sarcasm and Contempt:** They may use sarcasm, mockery, or expressions of disgust to convey their disapproval.
- **Yelling and Screaming:** They may raise their voice, yell, or scream.

During the outburst, the OCPD individual is often unreachable. They are flooded with emotion and unable to engage in a rational conversation.

The Aftermath: The Restoration of Control

After the outburst, the OCPD individual may feel a sense of relief. The anger has dissipated the anxiety. They may return to their calm demeanor as if nothing happened, expecting you to do the same.

They rarely apologize or take responsibility for their behavior. They genuinely believe their anger was justified by your mistake or the situation. The aftermath often leaves you feeling shaken, confused, and hurt.

The Intensity of the Reaction Often Being Disproportionate to the Event

One of the most confusing aspects of the OCPD anger cycle is the intensity of the reaction, which often seems completely disproportionate to the event.

You might spill a glass of milk, and they react as if you have committed a cardinal sin. You might be five minutes late, and they react as if you have betrayed their trust.

The Symbolic Meaning of the Trigger

To understand the disproportionate reaction, you have to understand the symbolic meaning of the trigger.

The spilled milk is not just a mess; it is a symbol of chaos, carelessness, and lack of control. The five minutes of lateness is not just a minor inconvenience; it is a symbol of disrespect and the unpredictability of the world.

The OCPD individual is not reacting to the event itself. They are reacting to the underlying threat that the event represents. They are reacting to the fear that their carefully constructed world is falling apart.

The Accumulation of Stress

The OCPD individual lives in a constant state of stress, driven by their relentless pursuit of perfection. They are constantly monitoring the environment for threats.

This chronic stress accumulates over time. They are like a pressure cooker. When a trigger occurs, it releases the pressure. The outburst is not just a reaction to the immediate event; it is a release of all the accumulated stress and frustration.

The Black-and-White Thinking

The black-and-white thinking that characterizes OCPD also contributes to the disproportionate reaction. They see things in extremes. A small mistake is not a minor flaw; it is a total failure. This distorted thinking magnifies the perceived threat and justifies the intense emotional reaction.

Case Example: The Ruined Dinner

Sarah spent the afternoon cooking a special dinner for her husband, Mark. She accidentally overcooked the vegetables slightly.

When Mark sat down to eat, he tasted the vegetables and frowned. "These are ruined," he declared. He pushed his plate away and launched into a lecture about the importance of precise cooking times.

Sarah was devastated. Mark's reaction was disproportionate. The vegetables were not ruined. But for Mark, they represented a failure of execution and a violation of his standards. His black-and-white thinking led him to categorize the entire meal as a failure.

Why They Are So Defensive and Unable to Apologize

In the aftermath of an outburst, what you long for most is an apology. But apologies are rare in an OCPD marriage. The OCPD individual is often intensely defensive and unable to admit wrongdoing.

The Ego-Syntonic Nature of OCPD

As we discussed earlier, OCPD is ego-syntonic. The individual believes their way is the right way.

To apologize would mean admitting they were wrong. It would mean acknowledging that their standards are too high or their reactions are excessive. This admission of wrongdoing is deeply threatening to the OCPD individual. It challenges their core identity.

The Fear of Shame

Shame is a powerful emotion that arises when we believe we are flawed or unworthy. The OCPD individual is driven by a deep-seated fear of shame. They strive for perfectionism as a way to avoid this painful experience.

Admitting wrongdoing triggers shame. It exposes their imperfections. To protect themselves from shame, they employ defense mechanisms like denial, rationalization, and projection.

The Defense Mechanisms

- **Denial:** They may simply deny that the outburst happened or minimize its severity. "I wasn't yelling."

- **Rationalization:** They may provide logical explanations for their behavior. "If I didn't get angry, nothing would ever get done right."

- **Projection:** They may project their own unacceptable feelings onto you, blaming you for the outburst. "I wouldn't have gotten angry if you hadn't been so careless."

These defense mechanisms protect them from the discomfort of shame and the responsibility of change.

DARVO: Deny, Attack, Reverse Victim and Offender

In some cases, the defensiveness may escalate into a pattern known as DARVO (Freyd, 1997). This is an acronym for Deny, Attack, and Reverse Victim and Offender. It is a manipulative tactic used to avoid accountability.

- **Deny:** They deny the behavior. ("I didn't yell.")
- **Attack:** They attack the credibility or character of the person confronting them. ("You are just saying that because you are too sensitive.")
- **Reverse Victim and Offender:** They claim that they are the real victim and that you are the offender. ("I am the one who has to deal with your constant mistakes. You are the one who is stressing me out.")

DARVO is highly effective at silencing the victim and shifting the blame. It leaves you feeling confused, guilty, and powerless.

The Impact of the Lack of Apology

The inability to apologize is incredibly damaging to the relationship. It prevents the repair of the rupture caused by the outburst. It leaves you feeling invalidated and resentful. It erodes trust and intimacy. You learn that you cannot rely on your partner to take responsibility for their actions or to care about your feelings.

Understanding these dynamics can help you depersonalize the anger and protect yourself from the emotional fallout. It can help you see the vulnerability beneath the rage and the fear beneath the control.

Understanding the Explosions

- The OCPD anger cycle is triggered by a perceived loss of control or error, leading to a rapid escalation from anxiety to anger.

- Anger is a secondary emotion that masks the primary emotion of fear—the fear of chaos, vulnerability, and error.

- The intensity of the reaction is often disproportionate to the event, driven by the symbolic meaning of the threat, accumulated stress, and black-and-white thinking.

- OCPD individuals are often defensive and unable to apologize because admitting wrongdoing threatens their core identity and triggers shame. They may use tactics like DARVO to avoid responsibility.

- Understanding the dynamics of the OCPD anger cycle is crucial for navigating these explosive situations and protecting your own well-being.

Chapter 9: The Essential First Step: Boundaries, Not Battles

Up until now, we've focused heavily on understanding the OCPD mindset. We've looked at the rigidity, the anxiety beneath the control, and the profound impact this has on you. Understanding is crucial. It provides context. But understanding alone won't change the dynamic in your marriage.

If you've been living in this pattern for a while, you've likely tried everything to make things better. You've argued, pleaded, explained, and compromised. You've tried to be more organized, more punctual, more perfect. You've tried to get them to see your perspective. And yet, nothing changes. The criticism continues. The control tightens.

This is exhausting, right? It leads to that sense of hopelessness we talked about.

If you want to shift the dynamic, you have to stop engaging in the same unwinnable battles. You have to shift your focus from trying to change *them* to trying to protect *yourself*. The essential first step in this process is implementing boundaries. Boundaries are the key to reclaiming your sanity and your power in this relationship. But they are often misunderstood, especially in the context of a controlling relationship.

Understanding That You Cannot Change Them, Only Your Response

This is perhaps the hardest truth to accept in any relationship, but it is absolutely critical in an OCPD marriage. **You cannot change your partner.**

You cannot convince them to be less rigid. You cannot argue them out of their anxiety. You cannot make them see the world the way you do.

Why? Because OCPD is a personality disorder. It is deeply ingrained. It is ego-syntonic, meaning they believe their way is the correct way. They are not motivated to change because they do not see themselves as the problem. They see you as the problem.

When you focus your energy on trying to change them, you are setting yourself up for failure and frustration. You are essentially banging your head against a brick wall. It hurts you, and it doesn't move the wall.

The Illusion of Control

We often believe that if we just find the right words, the right argument, the right timing, we can make them understand. We believe we can control their behavior. This is an illusion.

The only person you have control over is yourself. You control your responses, your choices, your behavior.

This realization can be initially terrifying. It means accepting the reality of the situation. It means grieving the loss of the partner you wished you had. But it is also incredibly empowering. When you stop trying to control the uncontrollable, you free up an enormous amount of energy. You can channel that energy into creating a life that is healthier and more peaceful for you.

Radical Acceptance

This shift requires what psychologists call *radical acceptance*. Radical acceptance means completely and totally accepting reality as it is, without judgment and without trying to change it (Linehan, 1993).

It does not mean you approve of their behavior. It does not mean you like it. It simply means you acknowledge that it is happening.

When you radically accept that your partner is rigid, critical, and controlling, you can stop being surprised and devastated every time they act that way. You can start making decisions based on reality, not wishful thinking.

Shifting Your Focus

When a conflict arises, instead of asking, "How can I make them stop criticizing me?" ask, "How can I respond in a way that protects my well-being?"

Instead of asking, "How can I get them to relax and be spontaneous?" ask, "How can I create space for spontaneity in my own life?"

This shift in focus changes everything. It moves you from a position of powerlessness to a position of agency.

The Difference Between Rules (Controlling Others) and Boundaries (Protecting Yourself)

This distinction is crucial. Your OCPD partner is very good at making rules. Rules are about controlling other people's behavior.

- "You must load the dishwasher this way."
- "You cannot spend money without my approval."
- "You should always be on time."

Rules are focused outward. They are attempts to impose order on the external world.

Boundaries, on the other hand, are about protecting yourself. They define what is acceptable and unacceptable behavior toward you. They are focused inward. They are about maintaining your own integrity and well-being (Tawwab, 2021).

Boundaries Define Your Space

Think of boundaries as a fence around your yard. The fence doesn't control what your neighbor does in their yard. It controls what comes into your yard.

A boundary is not an attempt to change your partner. It is a statement about what you will or will not do, or what you will or will not accept.

Let's look at the difference:

- **Rule:** "You need to stop criticizing me." (Focuses on their behavior, attempting to control them).
- **Boundary:** "If you criticize me, I will leave the room." (Focuses on your behavior, protecting yourself).
- **Rule:** "You have to stop working so much."
- **Boundary:** "I will not be available to discuss work-related issues after 7 PM."

See the difference? The boundary puts the power back in your hands. You are not waiting for them to change. You are taking action to protect yourself.

The Myth of Selfishness

Many people struggle with setting boundaries because they believe it is selfish, mean, or confrontational. This is especially true if you have been conditioned to prioritize others' needs above your own (the fawn response we discussed earlier).

But boundaries are not selfish. They are an essential component of healthy relationships. They create safety and trust. They allow you to show up as your authentic self without fear of judgment or violation.

In an OCPD marriage, boundaries are life-saving. They protect you from the emotional toll of constant criticism and control. They allow you to create space for your own needs and desires.

Identifying Your Non-Negotiables

Before you can set boundaries, you need to know what your boundaries are. This requires self-reflection and clarity about your needs, values, and limits.

Recognizing the Erosion

When you have been living in a controlling relationship for a long time, your boundaries may have eroded significantly. You may have normalized unacceptable behavior. You may have lost touch with your own needs.

The first step is to identify the areas where you feel most stressed, resentful, or violated. Resentment is a powerful signal that a boundary is needed (Tawwab, 2021). Where do you feel like you are walking on eggshells? What interactions leave you feeling drained or diminished?

Defining Your Needs

Once you have identified the problem areas, you need to define your needs. What do you need to feel safe, respected, and valued in the relationship?

Your needs might include:

- The need for emotional safety (freedom from excessive criticism).
- The need for autonomy (the ability to make your own decisions).
- The need for rest and relaxation (freedom from the pressure to be constantly productive).
- The need for financial independence.

Determining Your Non-Negotiables

Non-negotiables are the boundaries that are essential for your well-being. These are the deal-breakers.

Your non-negotiables might include:

- Zero tolerance for verbal abuse (yelling, name-calling, contempt).
- The right to make decisions about your own body and health.
- The right to maintain relationships with friends and family.

It is important to be realistic when defining your non-negotiables. You cannot demand that your partner become empathetic or flexible. But you can demand that they treat you with basic respect.

Starting Small

If the idea of setting boundaries feels overwhelming, start small. You don't have to tackle everything at once.

Identify one area where you can begin to assert yourself. Maybe it's about reclaiming your time in the evenings. Maybe it's about setting a limit on how much criticism you will tolerate.

Small successes build confidence and momentum.

Case Example: Reclaiming the Kitchen

Jenna, whom we met earlier, felt constantly criticized in the kitchen. She decided to set a boundary around cooking.

She said to her husband, Michael, "When I am cooking dinner, I need space to focus. I will no longer accept comments or corrections about my cooking methods while I am working. If you criticize me, I will stop cooking and you will be responsible for your own meal."

This boundary is clear, specific, and focuses on Jenna's behavior. It protects her from the stress of Michael's micromanagement.

How to Communicate Boundaries Clearly and Firmly

Setting boundaries is not just about knowing what they are; it's about communicating them effectively. This can be challenging with an OCPD partner, who is likely to resist any attempt to challenge their control.

Be Clear and Direct

Boundaries need to be communicated clearly and directly. Do not hint, suggest, or apologize. Be specific about the behavior that is unacceptable and the consequence if the boundary is violated.

Use simple, declarative sentences.

- "I will not participate in conversations where I am being yelled at."
- "I will be making my own decisions about how I spend my free time."

Stay Calm and Firm

The OCPD partner may react defensively or angrily when you set a boundary. They may try to engage you in a logic battle or guilt-trip you.

It is crucial to stay calm and firm. Do not get drawn into the drama. Repeat the boundary like a broken record if necessary. You do not need to justify, argue, defend, or explain (JADE) your boundary. Your boundary is valid simply because you have set it.

Choose the Right Time

It is generally best to communicate boundaries during a time of calm, rather than in the heat of the moment. This allows you to be more intentional and less reactive.

However, sometimes you need to set a boundary in the moment when a violation occurs.

Focus on "I" Statements

When communicating boundaries, focus on your own feelings and needs, rather than blaming or criticizing your partner. Use "I" statements.

- Instead of: "You are too controlling."
- Say: "I need to have autonomy over my own decisions."

The Importance of Consequences

A boundary without a consequence is just a request. The consequence is what gives the boundary teeth. It is the action you will take if the boundary is violated.

The consequence should be something that you have control over and that you are willing to follow through on. It should not be a punishment or a threat. It is simply the natural consequence of the boundary violation.

Examples of consequences:

- Leaving the room.
- Ending the conversation.
- Making a decision independently.

Preparing for the Inevitable Pushback and Testing

When you start setting boundaries, your OCPD partner will not likely respond with gratitude and understanding. They will likely push back. Hard.

This is because your boundaries threaten their sense of control and their established power dynamic. They will try to restore the status quo.

The Extinction Burst

When a behavior that has been reinforced (in this case, their control being reinforced by your compliance) is no longer reinforced, the behavior often gets worse before it gets better. This is known as an *extinction burst*.

Your partner may escalate their controlling behaviors in an attempt to force you back into compliance. They may become more critical, more demanding, or more angry.

This is the most critical phase of boundary setting. You must hold firm. If you give in during the extinction burst, you teach them that if they just push hard enough, they will get their way.

The Testing Phase

Your partner will test your boundaries repeatedly to see if you are serious. They will try to find loopholes or exceptions.

They may use various tactics to undermine your boundaries:

- **Guilt-tripping:** "How could you do this to me after all I've done for you?"
- **Gaslighting:** "You're being unreasonable. You're overreacting."
- **Victimhood:** "You're hurting me. You're abandoning me."
- **Logic battles:** "Your boundary is illogical. Let me explain why."

The Importance of Consistency

Consistency is key. You must follow through on your consequences every single time the boundary is violated. If you are inconsistent, you send the message that the boundary is negotiable.

Seeking Support

Setting boundaries in a controlling relationship is incredibly difficult. You do not have to do it alone. Seek support from friends, family, or a therapist who understands the dynamics of OCPD.

Support can provide validation, encouragement, and accountability. It can help you stay strong during the challenging phases of pushback and testing.

Setting boundaries is a process, not a one-time event. It requires courage, consistency, and self-compassion. But it is the essential first step toward creating a healthier and more balanced relationship.

Taking the First Step

- Accepting that you cannot change your OCPD partner, only your response, is the foundation for change. This requires radical acceptance.

- Boundaries are about protecting yourself, not controlling others. They define what is acceptable and unacceptable behavior toward you.

- Identifying your non-negotiables requires self-reflection and clarity about your needs and limits. Start small and build momentum.

- Communicate boundaries clearly, firmly, and calmly. Use "I" statements and define clear consequences.

- Prepare for pushback, including extinction bursts (escalation of behavior) and testing. Consistency is key to success.

- Seek support from others who understand the challenges of setting boundaries in a controlling relationship.

Chapter 10: De-escalation and Effective Communication

In an ideal world, communication in a marriage would be open, honest, and respectful. In an OCPD marriage, communication is often a minefield. The OCPD partner's rigidity, defensiveness, and need for control make it incredibly difficult to have a productive conversation.

You try to express your feelings, and you are met with criticism. You try to offer a different perspective, and you are drawn into an endless debate. You try to resolve a conflict, and you end up feeling more frustrated and disconnected than before.

If you want to survive in an OCPD marriage, you need a different approach to communication. You need strategies that allow you to express yourself clearly and effectively, while also protecting yourself from the emotional fallout of unproductive arguments.

This chapter is about de-escalation and effective communication. It's about learning how to navigate the minefield without getting blown up.

Techniques for Not Engaging in the "Logic Battle" (You Will Never Win)

We've talked about the "logic battle" before. This is the endless debate about the "right way" to do things, the "objective facts" of the situation, and the "logical" solution to the problem.

The OCPD partner is a master of the logic battle. They use their intellect and verbal skills to overwhelm you and shut down your perspective. They genuinely believe their reasoning is superior.

Here's the hard truth: You will never win the logic battle.

Why? Because the argument is not actually about logic. It is about control and anxiety. The OCPD partner uses logic as a defense mechanism to maintain their sense of order and superiority.

When you engage in the logic battle, you are playing their game, by their rules. You are reinforcing the idea that the argument is about facts, when it is actually about feelings and values.

Disengaging from the Content

The key to avoiding the logic battle is to disengage from the content of the argument and focus on the process.

Stop trying to convince them that your way is better. Stop trying to prove them wrong. Stop defending your choices.

Instead, focus on how the conversation is happening. Are you being heard? Are you being respected? Is the conversation productive?

The Power of "I Understand"

One powerful technique for disengaging from the logic battle is to use the phrase "I understand."

This does not mean you agree with them. It simply means you acknowledge their perspective.

When they launch into a lecture about the correct way to load the dishwasher, instead of arguing about the efficiency of your method, simply say:

- "I understand that you prefer it done that way."
- "I hear your perspective on this."

This validates their need to be heard without accepting their premise that their way is the only right way. It often takes the wind out of their sails because there is nothing left to argue about.

Avoiding JADE (Justify, Argue, Defend, Explain)

When you are criticized or challenged, it is natural to want to defend yourself. You want to justify your choices, argue your point, and explain your reasoning.

But in an OCPD marriage, these responses are counterproductive. They fuel the logic battle. They give the OCPD partner more ammunition to use against you.

The acronym JADE can help you remember what not to do:

- **Justify:** "I did it this way because..."
- **Argue:** "You're wrong. My way is better."
- **Defend:** "I'm not careless. I was just tired."
- **Explain:** "Let me explain why I made that choice."

When you feel the urge to JADE, stop. Take a breath. Remind yourself that you do not owe them an explanation for your choices. Your choices are valid simply because they are yours.

How to Validate Their Feelings Without Accepting Their Premises

Validation is a powerful tool for de-escalation. It involves acknowledging and accepting another person's feelings, without necessarily agreeing with them (Gottman & Silver, 2015).

The OCPD partner often feels misunderstood and attacked. They feel like they are the only one who cares about doing things correctly. When you validate their feelings, you can reduce their defensiveness and create space for a more productive conversation.

Identifying the Underlying Emotion

To validate their feelings, you need to identify the underlying emotion beneath their criticism or anger. Often, the emotion is anxiety, fear, or frustration.

When they criticize you for being late, the underlying emotion might be anxiety about the disruption to their schedule.

When they lecture you about spending money, the underlying emotion might be fear about financial insecurity.

Validating Statements

Once you have identified the emotion, you can offer a validating statement.

- "I can see that you are feeling very anxious about the schedule."
- "It sounds like you are worried about our finances."
- "I understand that this is important to you."

These statements acknowledge their emotional experience without validating their distorted thinking or accepting their criticism.

The "Yes, And" Technique

The "Yes, And" technique can be helpful for validating their perspective while also asserting your own.

- "Yes, I understand that you prefer the towels folded this way. And, I prefer to fold them my way."
- "Yes, I hear that you are worried about the cost. And, I believe this purchase is necessary."

This technique allows you to acknowledge their reality without sacrificing your own.

Case Example: The Thermostat War

Mark (OCPD) likes the house kept at 68 degrees Fahrenheit to save money. Sarah prefers it at 70 degrees because she feels cold.

Mark constantly turns the thermostat down and lectures Sarah about the cost of heating.

Instead of arguing about the cost (the logic battle), Sarah decides to validate Mark's feelings.

Sarah: "I understand that you are worried about the heating bill and want to save money (validation). And, I am cold and uncomfortable at 68 degrees (asserting her need). I would like to find a compromise that works for both of us."

By validating Mark's concern, Sarah reduces his defensiveness and opens the door for a conversation about a solution.

Using "I" Statements vs. "You" Accusations

When you are feeling frustrated or angry, it is easy to fall into the trap of using "You" accusations.

- "You are always criticizing me."
- "You never listen to me."
- "You are so controlling."

These statements attack the other person's character and immediately put them on the defensive. They escalate the conflict and shut down communication.

"I" statements, on the other hand, focus on your own feelings and experiences. They allow you to express yourself without blaming or accusing the other person (Gottman & Silver, 2015).

The Structure of an "I" Statement

A classic "I" statement has three parts:

1. **I feel...** (Your emotion)
2. **When...** (The specific behavior or situation)
3. **Because...** (The impact on you)

Let's look at how to transform "You" accusations into "I" statements:

- Instead of: "You are always criticizing me."

- Say: "I feel hurt when you comment on the way I do the chores because it makes me feel incompetent."

- Instead of: "You never listen to me."

- Say: "I feel frustrated when you interrupt me because it makes me feel like my perspective doesn't matter."

The Challenge with OCPD

While "I" statements are generally effective, they can be challenging with an OCPD partner. The OCPD individual's lack of empathy and defensiveness means they may still dismiss your feelings or turn the conversation back to your perceived flaws.

They might respond to your "I" statement with:

- "You shouldn't feel hurt. I'm just trying to help." (Gaslighting)

- "If you did the chores correctly, I wouldn't have to comment." (Blame-shifting)

If this happens, do not get drawn into a debate about the validity of your feelings. Simply restate your boundary.

"I understand that you are trying to help. However, I will not continue this conversation if you are criticizing me."

The goal of using "I" statements is not necessarily to change their behavior, but to express yourself authentically and assert your boundaries.

When and How to Walk Away from an Unproductive Argument

Sometimes, the most effective communication strategy is to stop communicating. When a conversation becomes unproductive, escalating, or abusive, the healthiest thing you can do is walk away.

Recognizing the Signs of an Unproductive Argument

An argument is unproductive when:

- It is going in circles, repeating the same points over and over.
- It is escalating in intensity, with yelling, screaming, or name-calling.
- You are feeling overwhelmed, confused, or unsafe.
- The focus has shifted from the issue at hand to personal attacks.

When you recognize these signs, it is time to disengage.

The "Time-Out" Technique

The "time-out" technique is a structured way to walk away from an unproductive argument (Gottman & Silver, 2015).

1. **Signal the need for a break:** Use a pre-agreed-upon phrase or gesture to signal that you need a break.
    - "I need a time-out."
    - "I'm feeling overwhelmed. I need a break."
2. **Disengage:** Stop talking and physically leave the room.
3. **Self-soothe:** During the break, focus on calming your nervous system. Take deep breaths, go for a walk, listen to music. The break should last at least 20 minutes to allow your physiological arousal to decrease.
4. **Return (Maybe):** After the break, you can decide whether to return to the conversation or let it go.

Dealing with Resistance

The OCPD partner may resist your attempts to walk away. They may follow you, block your path, or demand that you continue the conversation.

This is where your boundaries are crucial. You have the right to disengage from an unproductive argument.

Restate your boundary firmly and calmly.

- "I am willing to discuss this later when we are both calm. But I will not continue this conversation now."

If they persist, continue to walk away. Your safety and well-being are the priority.

The Power of Silence

Walking away is not a sign of weakness. It is a sign of strength and self-control. It is a refusal to participate in a dynamic that is damaging to you.

Silence can be a powerful tool. It creates space for reflection and de-escalation. It sends the message that you will not engage in destructive communication patterns.

Effective communication in an OCPD marriage is not about finding the perfect words to fix the relationship. It is about finding the right strategies to protect yourself and maintain your integrity. By learning to disengage from the logic battle, validate without agreeing, use "I" statements, and walk away when necessary, you can begin to change the dynamic of your communication and create a healthier space for yourself.

Navigating the Conversation

- Avoid the "logic battle" by disengaging from the content and focusing on the process. You will never convince them that they are wrong.

- Do not JADE (Justify, Argue, Defend, Explain). This only fuels the conflict.

- Validate their feelings without accepting their premises. Acknowledge their emotional experience without agreeing with their distorted thinking.

- Use "I" statements to express your feelings and needs without blaming or accusing.

- Walk away from unproductive arguments. Use the "time-out" technique to de-escalate the conflict and protect your well-being.

- Effective communication in an OCPD marriage is about protecting yourself, not fixing your partner.

Chapter 11: Navigating the Daily Grind: Specific Pain Points

The challenges of living with an OCPD partner are often most acute in the daily grind. The rigidity, perfectionism, and control permeate every aspect of domestic life, turning mundane tasks into potential battlegrounds.

We've covered the foundational strategies of setting boundaries and effective communication. Now, let's apply these strategies to the specific pain points that often arise in OCPD marriages. This chapter is about practical solutions for managing the daily grind and creating a more peaceful coexistence.

Managing Finances: Dealing with Extreme Frugality or Financial Control

Money is a major source of conflict in many marriages. In an OCPD marriage, the conflict is often exacerbated by the OCPD partner's extreme frugality and need for financial control.

The OCPD partner often views money as something to be hoarded for future catastrophes. They may impose strict budgets, monitor your spending obsessively, and criticize your purchases.

The Need for Financial Autonomy

The first step in managing financial conflict is to establish a degree of financial autonomy. You need to have access to money and the ability to make financial decisions independently.

If your partner controls all the finances, this can be challenging. But it is crucial for your well-being and empowerment.

Strategies for Creating Autonomy

- **Separate Accounts:** If possible, maintain separate bank accounts. This allows you to manage your own money without interference.

- **The "Yours, Mine, and Ours" System:** A common approach is to have a joint account for shared expenses and separate accounts for personal spending. This requires negotiation and agreement on how shared expenses are managed.

- **Negotiating a Personal Allowance:** If separate accounts are not feasible, negotiate a personal allowance that you can spend without oversight.

Setting Boundaries Around Financial Discussions

The OCPD partner may try to engage you in endless discussions about finances, budgets, and spending. You need to set boundaries around these conversations.

- **Scheduled Financial Meetings:** Agree to discuss finances at a specific time each week or month. This contains the discussions and prevents them from bleeding into every aspect of your life.

- **Time Limits:** Set a time limit for these meetings. When the time is up, the discussion is over.

- **Rules of Engagement:** Establish rules for these discussions, such as no criticism, no yelling, and a focus on solutions rather than blame.

Dealing with Frugality

The OCPD partner's frugality can be difficult to live with, especially if it impacts your quality of life.

- **Prioritize Your Needs:** Identify the areas where their frugality is unacceptable to you. Maybe it's about the quality of food, the temperature of the house, or the ability to engage in leisure activities.

- **Negotiate Compromises:** Try to find compromises that respect their need for saving while also meeting your needs.
- **Use Your Own Money:** If you have separate finances, use your own money for the things that are important to you.

Recognizing Financial Abuse

In extreme cases, financial control can cross the line into financial abuse. This includes restricting access to money, preventing you from working, or forcing you to account for every penny you spend. If you are experiencing financial abuse, it is crucial to seek help from a professional organization that specializes in domestic violence.

Chores and Housework: Creating Zones of Control or Agreeing to Disagree

Chores and housework are another major battleground in OCPD marriages. The OCPD partner's perfectionism and "One Right Way" mentality can turn simple tasks into sources of intense conflict.

The Futility of Perfection

The first step is to accept that you will never meet their standards of perfection. Stop trying. It is an unwinnable game.

Instead, focus on finding a way to manage the household that minimizes conflict and stress.

The "Zones of Control" Strategy

One effective strategy is to create "zones of control." This means dividing the household tasks and responsibilities, and agreeing that each person has full autonomy over their assigned areas.

- **Divide and Conquer:** Divide the tasks based on preferences and availability. Maybe one person is responsible for the kitchen, and the other is responsible for the laundry.
- **The Rule of Non-Interference:** The key to this strategy is the rule of non-interference. You agree not to comment on,

criticize, or correct the other person's work in their assigned zone.

This strategy allows the OCPD partner to maintain control over certain areas, satisfying their need for order, while also creating space for you to manage your areas without interference.

Agreeing to Disagree

In areas where shared responsibility is unavoidable, you may need to agree to disagree about the "right way" to do things.

- **Defining "Good Enough":** Negotiate a standard of "good enough" that is acceptable to both of you. This will likely require the OCPD partner to tolerate some degree of imperfection.
- **The "My Space, My Rules" Approach:** In shared spaces, you can establish boundaries around your own belongings and areas. For example, "This is my desk, and I will organize it my way."

Outsourcing

If finances allow, outsourcing household tasks can be a game-changer. Hiring a cleaning service, using a laundry service, or getting meal delivery kits can reduce the burden of housework and eliminate sources of conflict.

Case Example: The Laundry Truce

Tom (OCPD) insisted that the laundry be folded in a very specific way. Lisa found his method time-consuming and unnecessary. They fought about it constantly.

They decided to implement the "zones of control" strategy. Lisa agreed to be responsible for the laundry, and Tom agreed not to comment on how she folded it.

This required Tom to tolerate the "imperfectly" folded towels. But it also eliminated the daily conflict and freed up Lisa's time and energy.

Parenting: Protecting Children from Perfectionistic Expectations

Parenting with an OCPD partner is incredibly challenging. The OCPD parent often has rigid rules, high expectations, and a critical parenting style. This can be damaging to children's self-esteem and emotional development.

Your primary role is to protect your children from the harmful effects of the OCPD parent's rigidity and perfectionism.

Creating a Safe Emotional Environment

You need to create a safe emotional environment where your children feel loved, accepted, and validated.

- **Unconditional Love:** Counteract the OCPD parent's conditional approval with unconditional love. Let your children know that you love them no matter what, mistakes and all.

- **Validating Feelings:** Validate your children's feelings, especially when they are dismissed by the OCPD parent. "I understand that you are feeling sad that Daddy criticized your drawing."

- **Encouraging Play and Spontaneity:** Create opportunities for unstructured play, creativity, and spontaneity. Protect your children from the pressure to be constantly productive.

Setting Boundaries Around Parenting

You need to set boundaries around the OCPD parent's parenting behaviors.

- **Zero Tolerance for Criticism:** Establish a zero-tolerance policy for excessive criticism, yelling, or shaming of the children.

- **Intervening When Necessary:** If the OCPD parent is being overly critical or controlling, intervene to protect the child. "I will not allow you to talk to our child that way."

- **Advocating for the Child's Needs:** Advocate for your child's needs, especially when they conflict with the OCPD parent's rigid expectations.

Parallel Parenting

In high-conflict situations, you may need to adopt a parallel parenting approach. This means minimizing communication and interaction between the parents, and maximizing each parent's autonomy over their own parenting time.

This is not ideal, but it can be necessary to protect the children from the conflict and stress of the OCPD dynamic.

Seeking Professional Help

If you are concerned about the impact of the OCPD parent's behavior on your children, seek professional help from a family therapist who has experience with personality disorders.

Social Life and Vacations: Managing Their Need to Over-Schedule and Inability to Relax

Social life and vacations are often sources of stress rather than relaxation in OCPD marriages. The OCPD partner's rigidity, inflexibility, and need to over-schedule can ruin the enjoyment of these activities.

Managing Social Situations

The OCPD partner may be uncomfortable in social situations, especially those that are unstructured or unpredictable. They may try to control the conversation, criticize others, or insist on leaving early.

- **Setting Expectations:** Before a social event, set expectations about the duration and nature of the activity.
- **Having an Escape Plan:** Have an escape plan in case the OCPD partner becomes overwhelmed or agitated.

- **Separate Social Lives:** It is okay to maintain a separate social life. You do not have to do everything together.

Navigating Vacations

Vacations can be particularly challenging. The OCPD partner may try to plan every detail of the trip, creating a rigid itinerary that leaves no room for spontaneity or relaxation.

- **Negotiating the Itinerary:** Negotiate the itinerary in advance, balancing their need for structure with your need for flexibility.
- **Scheduling Downtime:** Schedule downtime into the itinerary.
- **The "Divide and Conquer" Vacation:** Consider taking separate vacations or dividing the vacation time so that each person can engage in activities they enjoy.

Redefining Relaxation

The OCPD partner often struggles with relaxation. They may view downtime as wasteful or unproductive.

You need to redefine relaxation for yourself and create opportunities for rest and rejuvenation, regardless of their participation.

- **Prioritizing Your Needs:** Identify the activities that help you relax and prioritize them.
- **Creating Space for Yourself:** Create space in your daily life for relaxation, even if it means disengaging from your partner.

Managing the daily grind in an OCPD marriage requires a combination of boundaries, negotiation, and acceptance. By focusing on practical solutions and prioritizing your own well-being, you can create a more peaceful and sustainable life.

Managing Daily Life

- Manage financial conflict by establishing financial autonomy, setting boundaries around financial discussions, and recognizing the signs of financial abuse.

- Minimize conflict over chores by creating "zones of control," agreeing to disagree about standards, and outsourcing tasks when possible.

- Protect children from the OCPD parent's perfectionism by creating a safe emotional environment, setting boundaries around parenting behaviors, and considering parallel parenting if necessary.

- Navigate social life and vacations by managing expectations, negotiating itineraries, and prioritizing your own need for relaxation and spontaneity.

- Focus on practical solutions that minimize conflict and prioritize your well-being.

Chapter 12: Reclaiming Your Identity: Radical Self-Care

When you have been living in the shadow of OCPD for a long time, your world often shrinks. You become so focused on managing their rigidity, avoiding their criticism, and maintaining the fragile peace that you lose touch with yourself. Your identity becomes intertwined with their demands and expectations.

We talked earlier about the erosion of self-esteem and the loss of identity that often occurs in OCPD marriages. You may feel like a shell of your former self.

This final chapter is about the most important part of the survival guide: reclaiming your identity. It's about the process of rediscovering who you are, what you want, and how to live a fulfilling life, regardless of your partner's behavior.

This process requires what I call *radical self-care*. This is not just about bubble baths and massages. It is about the deep, intentional work of prioritizing your own well-being and reconnecting with your authentic self.

The Importance of Detaching Your Identity from Their Approval

The first step in reclaiming your identity is to detach your sense of self-worth from their approval.

In an OCPD marriage, you are constantly bombarded with the message that you are not good enough. The OCPD partner's criticism and perfectionism create a dynamic where you are always striving for validation that is rarely given.

If your self-esteem is dependent on their approval, you will always be miserable. You are giving them all the power over how you feel about yourself.

Internalizing Your Validation

You need to develop an internal locus of control. This means shifting your focus from external validation (their approval) to internal validation (your own values and standards).

Start by recognizing the internalized critical voice—the voice that sounds like them, telling you that you are wrong or inadequate. This is not your voice. It is their voice that you have adopted.

Challenge this critical voice. When you hear it, remind yourself:

- "I am good enough."
- "My opinion matters."
- "I have the right to make my own choices."

The Process of Differentiation

In psychological terms, this process is called *differentiation*. Differentiation is the ability to maintain your sense of self—your values, opinions, and desires—even when you are in a close relationship with someone who sees the world differently (Schnarch, 1997).

A differentiated person can agree to disagree without feeling threatened. They can maintain their emotional equilibrium even when their partner is upset. They can take responsibility for their own feelings and behaviors, without blaming others.

In an OCPD marriage, differentiation is essential for survival. It allows you to stay connected to your partner without losing yourself in their rigidity.

How to Differentiate

- **Know what you believe:** Get clear on your own values, opinions, and preferences.
- **Speak your truth:** Express yourself authentically, even if it means disagreeing with your partner.
- **Tolerate discomfort:** Differentiation often involves tolerating the discomfort of conflict and disapproval.
- **Maintain your boundaries:** Boundaries are the foundation of differentiation. They define where you end and they begin.

Case Example: Rediscovering Her Voice

Maria had always deferred to her husband David's opinions. She had adopted his political views, his social preferences, and even his style of dress.

As she began the process of differentiation, Maria started to explore her own interests. She started reading books that David disapproved of. She started expressing her own opinions in conversations.

David reacted defensively. He accused her of being rebellious and irrational. But Maria held firm. She realized that his disapproval was uncomfortable, but it was not unbearable. She realized that she could survive without his validation.

Building a Support System Outside the Marriage (Friends, Therapy)

Living with an OCPD partner is isolating. The constant criticism and control can make you feel ashamed and alone. You may have distanced yourself from friends and family because it was easier than explaining the reality of your marriage.

Rebuilding your support system is a crucial part of reclaiming your identity. You need people in your life who can offer validation, perspective, and encouragement.

The Need for External Validation

When you are in a relationship with someone who constantly invalidates your reality, you need external sources of validation. You need people who can remind you that you are not crazy, that your feelings are valid, and that you deserve to be treated with respect.

Reconnecting with Friends and Family

Reach out to friends and family members who you trust and who make you feel good about yourself. Be honest with them about what you are going through (to the extent that you feel safe and comfortable).

You may be surprised by how much support and understanding you receive.

Finding New Connections

If your existing social network is depleted, seek out new connections. Join a club, take a class, volunteer for a cause you care about. Look for communities where you can connect with like-minded people.

The Role of Therapy

Therapy is often essential for navigating the complexities of an OCPD marriage. A good therapist can provide a safe space to process your feelings, develop coping strategies, and rebuild your self-esteem.

It is important to find a therapist who has experience with personality disorders and the dynamics of controlling relationships.

Therapy is not about fixing your partner. It is about supporting you. It is about helping you reclaim your identity and make informed decisions about your future.

Support Groups

Support groups for partners of individuals with personality disorders can also be incredibly helpful. Connecting with others who share your experience can reduce isolation and provide valuable insights and resources.

Re-engaging with Hobbies and Interests They May Have Criticized

The OCPD partner often criticizes or dismisses hobbies and interests that they deem unproductive or frivolous. You may have given up activities you once enjoyed because it was easier than dealing with their disapproval.

Re-engaging with these activities is a powerful way to reconnect with your authentic self.

The Power of Play

Play, creativity, and leisure are essential for mental and emotional well-being. They provide a counterbalance to the stress and rigidity of the OCPD dynamic.

Think back to the activities you enjoyed before the relationship, or the activities you have always wanted to try.

- Did you love to paint, but stopped because it was too messy?
- Did you enjoy socializing, but stopped because your partner criticized your friends?
- Did you want to learn a new skill, but were afraid of making mistakes?

Reclaiming Your Space and Time

You need to reclaim space and time for your own interests. This may require setting boundaries around your schedule and your physical environment.

- Create a dedicated space in your home for your hobbies.
- Schedule time in your calendar for activities you enjoy.
- Do not apologize for taking time for yourself.

Embracing Joy

When you re-engage with your hobbies and interests, you invite joy back into your life. Joy is a powerful antidote to the negativity and depletion of the OCPD marriage.

It reminds you that life is more than just work, chores, and productivity. It reminds you that you deserve to experience pleasure and fulfillment.

The Permission to Be Imperfect and Prioritize Your Own Mental Health

The most radical act of self-care in an OCPD marriage is giving yourself permission to be imperfect.

The OCPD partner demands perfection. They hold you to impossible standards. They criticize your flaws and mistakes.

If you want to reclaim your identity, you must reject their perfectionism and embrace your humanity.

Embracing Imperfection

Perfectionism is a prison. It keeps you trapped in a cycle of anxiety and self-criticism.

Embracing imperfection means accepting that you are flawed, that you will make mistakes, and that that is okay.

- Allow yourself to do things "good enough."
- Allow yourself to be messy.
- Allow yourself to be spontaneous.

When you embrace imperfection, you free yourself from the tyranny of the OCPD standards. You reclaim your freedom and your authenticity.

Prioritizing Your Mental Health

Your mental health is your most valuable asset. You must prioritize it above all else.

This means:

- **Saying no:** Saying no to demands that are unreasonable or overwhelming.
- **Resting:** Getting enough sleep, taking breaks, and allowing yourself to relax.
- **Seeking help:** Reaching out for professional help when you need it.
- **Making hard choices:** Making decisions that protect your well-being, even if they are difficult or unpopular.

Prioritizing your mental health is not selfish. It is necessary for your survival.

The Journey of Reclamation

Reclaiming your identity is a journey, not a destination. It is a process of ongoing self-discovery and growth.

It requires courage, commitment, and self-compassion. There will be setbacks and challenges along the way. But every step you take toward reconnecting with your authentic self is a victory.

As you begin this journey, remember that you are worthy of love, respect, and fulfillment. You deserve to live a life that is aligned with your own values and desires. You deserve to be the author of your own story.

Reconnecting with Yourself

- Detach your identity and self-worth from your partner's approval. Develop an internal locus of control and practice differentiation.

- Build a strong support system outside the marriage, including friends, family, therapy, and support groups. External validation is crucial.

- Re-engage with hobbies and interests that bring you joy and fulfillment. Reclaim space and time for yourself.

- Give yourself permission to be imperfect. Reject the OCPD standards of perfectionism and embrace your humanity.

- Prioritize your mental health above all else. Practice radical self-care by setting boundaries, saying no, resting, and seeking help when needed.

- Reclaiming your identity is an ongoing journey of self-discovery and empowerment. You deserve to live an authentic and fulfilling life.

Chapter 13: Can an OCPD Person Change?

This is the million-dollar question, isn't it? It's the question that likely keeps you up at night, the one that holds the balance of your future. If they could just be a little less rigid, a little less critical, a little more emotionally present—then maybe this marriage could work.

It's natural to cling to the hope of change. You love them, or you once did, and you want the relationship to thrive. You see the good qualities—the dedication, the reliability, the intelligence—and you wish they weren't constantly overshadowed by the suffocating need for control.

But can a person with OCPD actually change?

The answer is complicated. It's not a simple yes or no. It's more of a "yes, but..."

Yes, change is possible. But when dealing with a personality disorder, it is difficult, slow, and often limited. Understanding the reality of OCPD treatment and setting realistic expectations is crucial for your own well-being. If you are waiting for a complete personality overhaul, you are likely setting yourself up for disappointment. But if you are looking for behavioral modifications that might make the relationship more manageable, that might be achievable—under the right circumstances.

The Reality of OCPD Treatment (The Difficulty Because They Don't See the Problem)

The single biggest obstacle to change in OCPD is the very nature of the disorder. As we discussed in Chapter 2, OCPD is *ego-syntonic*. This is the clinical term meaning the individual views their traits—

their rigidity, their perfectionism, their control—as virtues, not problems.

They genuinely believe their way is the correct, logical, and most ethical way to live. When conflicts arise, they do not look inward and think, "Maybe I'm being too controlling." They look outward and think, "Why is everyone else so disorganized, illogical, or lazy?"

The Motivation Barrier

Think about it: Why would you seek help for something you don't believe is broken?

This lack of internal motivation is why individuals with OCPD rarely seek therapy on their own (Diedrich & Voderholzer, 2015). They do not experience the distress and impairment that often drives people to therapy.

When individuals with OCPD do end up in therapy, it is usually because of external pressure. They are facing a crisis that their usual coping mechanisms cannot solve.

Common motivators include:

- **A Relationship Crisis:** Their partner threatens to leave or files for divorce. This is the most common reason.
- **A Career Crisis:** Their rigidity and inability to collaborate lead to problems at work, such as being fired or facing disciplinary action.
- **Secondary Symptoms:** The chronic stress of maintaining perfectionism can lead to burnout, anxiety, or depression. They may seek therapy for these symptoms without realizing they are connected to their personality structure.

Even when they do start therapy, their motivation is often focused on alleviating the external pressure, not on changing themselves. They might attend therapy to "fix" their partner, to prove they are right, or simply to get their partner off their back.

The Therapeutic Challenge

The therapeutic process itself is often challenging for individuals with OCPD. They tend to approach therapy with the same rigidity and control they apply to everything else.

- **Intellectualization:** They may focus heavily on logic and analysis, avoiding discussions about vulnerable emotions.
- **Control Battles:** They may try to control the therapy session, dictating the agenda, debating the therapist's approach, or trying to prove the therapist wrong.
- **Defensiveness:** They may become highly defensive when challenged, shifting blame and refusing to take responsibility.

A therapist working with an OCPD client needs to be skilled at navigating these defenses and building a trusting relationship without being drawn into the logic battle. This takes significant time and patience.

Case Example: Gary's "Therapy"

Gary's wife, Maria, gave him an ultimatum: go to therapy for his controlling behavior, or she was leaving. Gary reluctantly agreed. But in therapy, Gary spent the sessions complaining about Maria. He presented the therapist with a detailed list of her inefficiencies and flaws. He argued that his behavior was a logical response to her incompetence. When the therapist tried to explore Gary's underlying anxiety, he shut down, accusing the therapist of being biased. Gary quit after three sessions, declaring therapy a waste of time.

Gary's experience is common. The ego-syntonic nature of OCPD makes it incredibly difficult for the individual to engage meaningfully in the therapeutic process.

What Successful Therapy Looks Like (CBT, Psychodynamic Therapy)

Despite the challenges, successful therapy for OCPD is possible. When the individual is motivated—even if that motivation starts externally—therapy can help them develop greater self-awareness, flexibility, and emotional connection.

Several therapeutic approaches have shown promise.

Cognitive Behavioral Therapy (CBT)

CBT is a structured, goal-oriented approach focusing on identifying and changing distorted thinking patterns and behaviors. In OCPD treatment, CBT aims to challenge the rigid beliefs that drive perfectionism and control (Beck et al., 2015).

Key components of CBT for OCPD include:

- **Identifying Cognitive Distortions:** The therapist helps the individual identify their black-and-white thinking, catastrophizing, and "should" statements.

- **Challenging Rigid Beliefs:** The therapist helps them examine the evidence for their beliefs and develop more balanced perspectives. For example, challenging the belief that any mistake leads to disaster.

- **Behavioral Experiments:** The therapist encourages them to engage in experiments to test their rigid beliefs. For example, intentionally making a small mistake to see that the catastrophic outcome does not occur, or delegating a task and resisting the urge to micromanage.

- **Exposure to Imperfection:** Gradually exposing the individual to disorder or inefficiency and helping them tolerate the resulting anxiety without resorting to control.

Psychodynamic Therapy

Psychodynamic therapy is a deeper, more exploratory approach that focuses on understanding the underlying psychological forces and early experiences that drive behavior. It aims to explore the roots of the rigidity, the underlying anxiety and shame, and the defense mechanisms used to manage these painful emotions (Gabbard, 2014).

Key components of psychodynamic therapy for OCPD include:

- **Exploring Early Experiences:** The therapist helps the individual explore how their childhood experiences contributed to the development of their rigid personality structure.

- **Identifying Underlying Emotions:** Helping the individual identify and process vulnerable emotions (like fear or shame) that are masked by their control and anger.

- **Developing Emotional Awareness and Empathy:** Focusing on increasing understanding of their own emotions and the emotions of others.

- **Examining the Therapeutic Relationship:** Using the relationship with the therapist as a way to explore patterns of control and emotional avoidance.

Hallmarks of Successful Therapy

Successful therapy does not mean the person is "cured." It means they have developed the skills and awareness to manage their rigidity and improve their relationships.

Signs of success include increased flexibility, better emotional regulation, willingness to compromise, and taking responsibility for their actions rather than constantly blaming others.

Managing Expectations: Change Is Slow, Incremental, and Often Focuses on Behavior Modification, Not a Personality Overhaul

This is the most crucial point of this chapter. If you are waiting for your OCPD partner to wake up one day as a spontaneous, easygoing, emotionally expressive person, you are setting yourself up for heartbreak.

The goal of treatment for OCPD is generally behavior modification, not a personality overhaul.

The Nature of Change

Change in OCPD is slow and incremental. It is not a linear process. It's often two steps forward, one step back. Setbacks are common, especially during times of stress, as stress significantly reduces flexibility.

The Focus on Behavior

The most realistic goals focus on specific behaviors that damage the relationship.

Realistic goals might include:

- Reducing the frequency and intensity of criticism.
- Agreeing to compromise on specific issues (e.g., finances, chores).
- Learning to walk away from unproductive arguments.
- Increasing expressions of positive regard (e.g., saying "thank you" or offering compliments).

These behavioral changes can make a significant difference in the quality of the relationship, even if the underlying personality structure remains largely the same.

The Limits of Change

It is vital to acknowledge the limits of change. The OCPD individual will likely always have a preference for order and control. They will likely always struggle with spontaneity and deep emotional expression. They will not become a different person; they may become a more flexible, self-aware version of themselves.

Understanding this reality is crucial for making decisions about your relationship. You need to ask yourself: Is incremental behavioral change enough for me? Am I willing to accept the fundamental limitations of their personality?

If your partner is genuinely engaged in therapy and making a consistent effort, there may be hope for a healthier relationship. But if they refuse help, deny the problem, or make only superficial changes to keep you from leaving, you need to accept that this may be as good as it gets.

The Reality of Change

- The ego-syntonic nature of OCPD (they don't see the problem) is the biggest barrier to change. Motivation is often external (e.g., a relationship crisis).

- Successful therapy, often involving CBT or psychodynamic approaches, requires significant commitment and a skilled therapist.

- Change is slow, incremental, and focuses on behavior modification, not a complete personality overhaul.

- Managing expectations is crucial. The goal is improvement, not a cure.

- You must decide if the potential for incremental change is enough for you to remain in the relationship.

Chapter 14: Therapy and Intervention

When you are struggling in an OCPD marriage, therapy can feel like a beacon of hope. It offers the possibility of support, guidance, and tools for navigating the complex dynamics of the relationship.

But the path to getting help is often challenging. You might wonder whether to seek individual therapy, couples therapy, or both. You might struggle with how to approach your partner about therapy. And you may face the painful reality of what to do if they refuse help altogether.

This chapter is about understanding your therapeutic options and making informed decisions about the best path forward for you.

The Role of Individual Therapy for You

Let's start with the most important intervention: individual therapy for *you*.

Regardless of whether your partner ever agrees to therapy, seeking individual therapy for yourself is essential. This is not a sign of weakness; it is a sign of strength and a commitment to your own well-being.

Why You Need Therapy

Living with an OCPD partner takes a significant emotional toll. As we discussed in Chapter 5, you may be dealing with anxiety, depression, eroded self-esteem, and a loss of identity. You need a safe space to process these feelings and rebuild your sense of self.

The goals of individual therapy for you include:

- **Validation and Reality Testing:** A therapist can validate your experience, confirming that you are not "crazy" or "too sensitive." This is vital when you are being gaslit or constantly invalidated at home.

- **Rebuilding Self-Esteem:** Therapy helps you challenge the internalized critical voice (the one that sounds like your partner) and rebuild your confidence and self-worth.

- **Setting Boundaries:** A therapist is invaluable in helping you identify your non-negotiables and developing strategies for communicating and enforcing boundaries effectively.

- **Managing Emotional Distress:** Therapy provides tools for managing the anxiety, depression, and burnout common in these relationships.

- **Grieving and Acceptance:** Therapy helps you grieve the loss of the relationship you wished you had and move toward radical acceptance of your reality.

- **Decision Making:** A therapist provides a neutral space to explore your options and make informed decisions about the future of your relationship, without pressure or judgment.

Finding the Right Therapist

It is crucial to find a therapist who understands the dynamics of OCPD and controlling relationships. A therapist unfamiliar with these issues might inadvertently minimize your experience or offer advice that is counterproductive (like suggesting you try harder to meet their standards).

Look for a therapist who has experience with:

- Personality disorders (specifically OCPD or Narcissism, as the impact on the partner is similar).

- Emotional abuse and coercive control.

- Complex trauma (C-PTSD).

Don't be afraid to interview several therapists. You need someone who "gets it."

Pros and Cons of Couples Therapy with an OCPD Partner (and How to Find a Specialist)

Couples therapy is often the standard intervention for marital issues. But in the context of OCPD, it is complicated. It can be helpful under the right circumstances, but it can also be counterproductive or even damaging if not handled correctly.

The Pros of Couples Therapy

When both partners are motivated, couples therapy can offer benefits:

- **Improved Communication:** A skilled therapist can teach communication strategies and interrupt destructive patterns like the logic battle.
- **Negotiating Compromises:** A therapist can mediate negotiations about specific issues like finances or chores.
- **Increased Understanding:** A therapist can educate both partners about OCPD and its impact on the relationship dynamic.

The Cons and Risks of Couples Therapy

However, the risks are significant:

- **Controlling the Narrative:** The OCPD partner may try to dominate the session, debate the therapist, and focus the therapy on your perceived flaws.
- **Manipulation and Triangulation:** They may present as highly rational and articulate, attempting to manipulate the therapist into siding with them (triangulation). This can leave you feeling invalidated and betrayed by the therapist.

- **The Illusion of Progress:** The OCPD partner may perform well in therapy, saying the right things, but fail to implement changes at home.

- **Focusing on Compromise:** In a healthy relationship, compromise is essential. But in a controlling relationship, "compromise" often means the victim giving up more autonomy.

When Couples Therapy Is Contraindicated

Couples therapy is generally contraindicated (not recommended) when there is active emotional abuse or coercive control (Gottman & Silver, 2015). Therapy requires safety and trust. If you are afraid of your partner, if you fear retaliation for speaking honestly, or if they are using therapy to further their control, it can be damaging. In these situations, individual therapy is the safest approach.

Finding a Specialist

If you decide to pursue couples therapy, finding a therapist experienced with OCPD and high-conflict dynamics is **essential**.

You need a therapist who is:

- **Strong and Directive:** Able to manage the session, interrupt destructive patterns, and prevent the OCPD partner from dominating.

- **Knowledgeable About OCPD:** Understands the rigidity, defensiveness, and control dynamics.

- **Focused on Behavioral Change:** Prioritizes concrete behavioral changes over abstract discussions.

A skilled specialist can make the difference between a productive experience and a frustrating, damaging one.

How to Introduce the Idea of Therapy to a Reluctant Partner

Introducing therapy to an OCPD partner can be daunting. They are likely to resist the suggestion, viewing it as criticism or a threat.

Here are some strategies for approaching the conversation:

Use "I" Statements

Focus on your own feelings and needs, rather than blaming or diagnosing them.

- **Instead of:** "You need therapy because you are too controlling."
- **Say:** "I am struggling with the level of conflict in our relationship, and I need us to get help learning how to communicate better."

Frame It as a Tool for Improvement

The OCPD partner values efficiency and improvement. Frame therapy as a practical tool for achieving shared goals.

- "I think therapy could help us work together more effectively as a team and reduce the stress in our home."

Focus on the Relationship, Not the Diagnosis

Avoid using the label "OCPD." This will likely trigger defensiveness. Focus on the specific behaviors and relationship dynamics that are causing problems.

Be Prepared for Resistance

Your partner may react defensively or angrily. They may deny the problem or blame you. Stay calm and firm. Do not get drawn into a logic battle. Simply restate your need for help.

The Ultimatum (Use with Caution)

In some cases, you may need to issue an ultimatum: therapy as a condition of staying in the relationship. This should only be used as a last resort, when you are genuinely prepared to leave if they refuse. If you issue an ultimatum, you **must** be prepared to follow through.

What to Do When They Refuse Help and Blame You Entirely

Despite your best efforts, your partner may refuse to seek help and continue to blame you entirely. This is a painful reality, but it provides crucial information.

Accept Their Choice

Their refusal to seek help is a choice. Accepting this means letting go of the illusion that you can control or change their behavior.

Focus on Yourself

When your partner refuses to change, you must shift your focus entirely onto yourself.

- **Continue Your Own Therapy:** Your need for support is even greater now.
- **Strengthen Your Boundaries:** Use boundaries to protect yourself from their blame and control.
- **Reclaim Your Identity:** Focus on rebuilding your self-esteem, strengthening your support system, and finding joy outside the relationship.

Protect Yourself from Blame

The OCPD partner will likely escalate their blame when you start focusing on yourself. They may accuse you of being selfish or abandoning the relationship. Do not internalize this blame. You are not responsible for their choices.

The Decision Point

When your partner refuses to seek help and continues to engage in damaging behaviors, you arrive at a decision point. You must decide whether you can live with the relationship as it is, or whether you need to take steps to protect your own well-being—even if that means leaving.

We will explore this difficult decision in the next chapter.

Seeking Support

- Individual therapy for you is essential for rebuilding self-esteem, setting boundaries, and making informed decisions.

- Couples therapy can be risky and is contraindicated if abuse is present. If pursued, finding a specialist in OCPD and high conflict is crucial.

- When introducing therapy, use "I" statements, focus on the relationship dynamic, and frame it as a tool for improvement.

- If your partner refuses help, accept their choice, focus on your own healing, and protect yourself from blame.

- Their refusal to seek help brings you to a critical decision point about the future of the marriage.

Chapter 15: The Decision Point: Knowing When to Walk Away

This is likely the hardest chapter in this book. It addresses the agonizing decision of whether to stay or leave your marriage.

You have likely tried everything. You've read the books, attended therapy, set boundaries, and worked on your communication. And yet, the relationship may still be defined by conflict, control, and emotional distance. You may feel trapped, exhausted, and hopeless. You may love your partner, but you may also realize that the relationship is slowly destroying you.

The decision to leave is never easy. It is fraught with guilt, fear, and uncertainty. But in some cases, it is the healthiest and most courageous choice you can make.

This chapter is about how to know when it is time to walk away. It is about recognizing the signs that the relationship is unsalvageable and making a plan for separation that protects your safety and well-being.

When Love Is Not Enough: Recognizing Emotional Abuse and Coercive Control

"But I love him/her." This is often what keeps people tethered to painful relationships. We are taught that love conquers all. But love is not enough. A healthy relationship also requires respect, trust, safety, and emotional connection.

In many OCPD marriages, the dynamics of control and criticism cross the line into emotional abuse and coercive control. Recognizing these patterns is crucial.

Emotional Abuse: The Erosion of Self

Emotional abuse is a pattern of behavior that attacks your sense of self-worth and emotional well-being. It is often subtle and insidious.

Signs of emotional abuse include:

- **Constant Criticism:** Attacks on your character, competence, or appearance.
- **Contempt:** Mockery, sarcasm, eye-rolling, or expressions of disgust.
- **Gaslighting:** Making you doubt your own memory, perception, or sanity.
- **Blame-Shifting:** Refusing to take responsibility and blaming you for everything that goes wrong.
- **Emotional Withholding:** Refusing affection, empathy, or connection as a form of punishment.
- **Unreasonable Demands:** Expecting perfection and punishing you for falling short.

Emotional abuse is deeply damaging. It isolates you, erodes your self-esteem, and makes you feel powerless.

Coercive Control: The Invisible Cage

Coercive control is a broader pattern of behavior aimed at dominating a partner by eroding their freedom and autonomy (Stark, 2007). It creates an invisible cage around the victim. OCPD traits often overlap significantly with the tactics of coercive control.

- **Micromanagement:** Controlling every detail of your life, justified by efficiency or "correctness."
- **Isolation:** Making it difficult to see friends or family because they criticize your relationships or make socializing stressful.

- **Financial Control:** Restricting access to money, imposing strict budgets, or demanding accountability for every penny spent, justified by frugality.
- **Rigid Rule-Setting:** Imposing rigid rules that you must follow, with severe consequences (anger or the silent treatment) for disobedience.

Coercive control is not about isolated incidents. It is a pervasive pattern of domination. When the relationship crosses the line from difficult to abusive, the focus must shift from improving the relationship to protecting your safety and sanity.

Assessing the Long-Term Impact on Your Mental Health and Children

When deciding whether to stay or leave, you must consider the long-term impact of the relationship on your health and the well-being of your children.

The Toll on Your Health

Living in a state of chronic stress and emotional deprivation takes a heavy toll. The constant walking on eggshells keeps your nervous system in a state of high alert.

- **Mental Health Issues:** Anxiety, depression, burnout, and Complex Trauma (C-PTSD) are common.
- **Physical Health Issues:** Chronic stress manifests physically, leading to chronic pain, autoimmune disorders, cardiovascular problems, and sleep disturbances. As Van der Kolk (2014) explains, the body keeps the score of the trauma we endure.

If the cost of staying in the relationship is your health, the price is too high.

The Impact on Children

If you have children, consider the impact of the OCPD dynamic on their development. Children who grow up in environments characterized by rigidity, criticism, and high conflict are at higher risk for:

- **Anxiety and Low Self-Esteem:** They internalize the criticism and believe they are never good enough.

- **Perfectionism:** They may develop their own rigid patterns or become paralyzed by the fear of failure.

- **People-Pleasing:** They may learn to suppress their own needs and feelings (the fawn response) to avoid conflict.

Staying together "for the sake of the children" often backfires. You are modeling an unhealthy relationship dynamic. Sometimes, the most loving thing you can do for your children is to leave and create a peaceful, stable home.

The Signs That the Relationship Is Unsalvageable

How do you know when you have reached the point of no return? Here are some signs that the relationship may be unsalvageable:

1. **Refusal to Change or Take Responsibility:** Your partner refuses to acknowledge the problem, refuses to seek help, and continues to blame you entirely.

2. **Profound Lack of Empathy:** They show a consistent inability or unwillingness to understand the impact of their behavior on you.

3. **Presence of Abuse:** The relationship is characterized by emotional abuse or coercive control. Your safety and autonomy are compromised.

4. **Complete Burnout and Hopelessness:** You have nothing left to give. You feel empty, numb, and see no path forward.

5. **Deteriorating Health:** Your mental or physical health is suffering significantly due to the relationship stress.

You need to step back and assess the situation honestly. Is this the life you want?

Making a Plan for Separation with a High-Conflict Personality

If you decide to leave, you must plan carefully. Separating from an OCPD partner can be extremely challenging. They often react poorly to the loss of control that separation represents. They are likely to be high-conflict, angry, vindictive, or litigious.

The Importance of Preparation

Preparation is key. Do not announce your decision until you have a plan in place.

Key Steps in Preparation

- **Documentation:** Document everything. Keep a record of incidents of abuse, control, and criticism. Save emails and text messages. This documentation is crucial for the legal process.

- **Financial Planning:** Gather all financial documents (bank statements, tax returns, investment accounts). Open a separate bank account in your own name. Start saving an emergency fund.

- **Legal Counsel:** Consult with a lawyer experienced in high-conflict divorce and personality disorders (Eddy, 2011). They can advise you on your rights and help develop a strategy.

- **Emotional Support:** Build a strong support system (friends, family, therapist) to help you through the emotional fallout.

- **Safety Planning:** If you are concerned about your safety, develop a safety plan. This may include changing locks, altering routines, and notifying your workplace or a domestic violence shelter.

Managing the Separation Process

During the separation process, minimize direct contact and establish firm boundaries.

- **Limited Communication:** Limit communication to essential matters (logistics, parenting). Use email or a co-parenting app to keep a record and reduce emotional engagement.

- **Parallel Parenting:** If you have children, establish a parallel parenting plan that minimizes interaction and conflict between parents.

- **Self-Care:** Prioritize your self-care rigorously during this incredibly stressful time.

Leaving an OCPD marriage is a difficult journey. But it is also an opportunity for profound healing and growth. Once free from the constant control, you can begin rebuilding your life on your own terms.

The Path Forward

- Recognize the signs of emotional abuse and coercive control. Love is not enough when respect and safety are absent.

- Assess the long-term impact on your mental and physical health and the well-being of your children.

- Identify the signs that the relationship is unsalvageable, including refusal to change, lack of empathy, and the presence of abuse.

- If you decide to leave, make a strategic plan for separation. Preparation is essential when dealing with a high-conflict personality.

- Leaving is a difficult journey, but it opens the door to healing, growth, and a peaceful, authentic life.

Conclusion: Your Life, Your Rules

We have covered a significant amount of ground in this book. We started by exploring the rigid and confusing world of OCPD—the perfectionism, the control, the hidden anxiety. We examined the profound impact these behaviors have on you—the erosion of self-esteem, the loneliness, the exhaustion of walking on eggshells.

And we explored strategies for surviving and thriving in this challenging relationship—setting boundaries, communicating effectively, managing the daily grind, and, ultimately, reclaiming your identity.

Navigating a marriage with an OCPD partner is one of the most difficult challenges you may ever face. It requires a level of strength, resilience, and self-awareness you may not have known you possessed.

As we conclude this guide, I want to leave you with a final message of empowerment and hope.

Recap of the Most Critical Survival Strategies

The strategies discussed are not a quick fix. They won't transform your partner. But they can transform you and how you navigate this relationship.

The most critical survival strategies are:

- **Radical Acceptance:** Accepting the reality of your partner's limitations. Letting go of the fantasy that you can change them.
- **Boundaries, Not Battles:** Shifting your focus from trying to control their behavior to protecting your own well-being. Setting clear boundaries and enforcing them consistently.

- **Disengaging from the Logic Battle:** Refusing to engage in unproductive arguments about the "right way." Do not JADE (Justify, Argue, Defend, Explain).

- **Reclaiming Your Identity (Differentiation):** Detaching your self-worth from their approval. Building a support system and finding joy outside the marriage.

- **Radical Self-Care:** Prioritizing your mental and physical health above all else. Giving yourself permission to be imperfect.

These strategies are the foundation for creating a life aligned with your own values, regardless of your partner's behavior.

Empowerment and the Realization That You Deserve Peace

When you have lived in a controlling relationship for a long time, you may start to believe the criticism. You may believe you are inadequate or unworthy.

I want to remind you that this is not the truth.

You are worthy of love, respect, and dignity. You deserve to feel safe and valued. You deserve autonomy over your own life. **You deserve peace.**

Empowerment comes from recognizing your worth and taking action to protect it. It comes from realizing that while you cannot control their behavior, you absolutely control your response. You can choose boundaries. You can choose to speak your truth. You can choose your own well-being.

A Final Message of Hope for Healing, Regardless of the Relationship's Outcome

The future of your relationship may be uncertain. You may choose to stay and work on creating a healthier dynamic. Or you may choose to leave and create a new life for yourself.

There is no single right answer. The decision is yours alone.

But regardless of the outcome of the relationship, know this: Healing is possible.

You can heal from the emotional toll of the OCPD marriage. You can rebuild your self-esteem and reclaim your identity. You can create a life filled with joy, connection, and meaning.

The journey may be long and difficult, but you have the strength and resilience to navigate it. You have the wisdom to make the choices that are right for you.

Thank you for allowing me to accompany you on this journey. I wish you clarity, courage, and peace as you move forward.

Appendix A: OCPD Symptom Checklist

This checklist is based on the diagnostic criteria for Obsessive-Compulsive Personality Disorder (OCPD) in the DSM-5-TR (American Psychiatric Association, 2022), simplified for the layperson. A diagnosis of OCPD requires a pervasive pattern of preoccupation with orderliness, perfectionism, and control, indicated by at least four of the following eight traits.

Does your partner...

1. **Focus excessively on details, rules, lists, organization, or schedules, to the point that the main point of the activity is lost?** (e.g., spending more time planning a vacation than enjoying it).

2. **Exhibit perfectionism that interferes with getting things done?** (e.g., unable to finish a project because it is not yet "perfect").

3. **Show excessive devotion to work and productivity, to the exclusion of leisure activities and relationships?** (e.g., constantly working, viewing relaxation as wasteful).

4. **Act overly conscientious, scrupulous, and inflexible about matters of morality, ethics, or values?** (e.g., rigid adherence to rules, judgmental of others' mistakes).

5. **Have difficulty discarding worn-out or worthless objects, even when they have no sentimental value?** (e.g., hoarding items "just in case").

6. **Show reluctance to delegate tasks or work with others unless they submit to exactly their way of doing things?** (e.g., micromanaging, refusing help).

7. **Adopt a miserly spending style; viewing money as something to be hoarded for future catastrophes?** (e.g., extreme frugality, financial control).

8. **Show rigidity and stubbornness?** (e.g., inability to compromise, insisting their way is the only right way).

This checklist is for informational purposes only and is not a substitute for a professional diagnosis.

Appendix B: Boundary Setting Worksheet and Scripts

Boundary Setting Worksheet

1. Identify the Problem Area: (Where do you feel most stressed or resentful? e.g., chores, criticism, finances).

   _____

2. Define Your Need: (What do you need to feel safe/respected? e.g., autonomy, emotional safety).

   _____

3. Determine Your Boundary: (What specific behavior is unacceptable? e.g., yelling, criticizing my cooking).

   _____

4. Define the Consequence: (What action will YOU take if the boundary is violated? e.g., leave the room, end the conversation).

   _____

5. Communicate the Boundary: (Write a clear, firm "I" statement).

   _____

Boundary Scripts

- **Criticism:** "I will not continue this conversation if you are criticizing me. If you continue, I will leave the room."

- **Micromanagement:** "I appreciate your input, but I will handle this task my way. If you try to interfere, I will ask you to leave the area."
- **Unproductive Arguments (Time-Out):** "I'm feeling overwhelmed and need a break. I will not continue this discussion right now. I am taking a time-out."
- **Workaholism:** "I will not be available to discuss work-related issues after 7 PM. If you bring up work, I will remind you of this boundary and disengage."

Appendix C: Resources

Therapist Directories

- **Psychology Today (psychologytoday.com):** Allows filtering by specialty (including personality disorders, trauma, and emotional abuse).
- **GoodTherapy (goodtherapy.org):** Directory focusing on ethical therapy practices.
- **The International OCD Foundation (IOCDF.org):** Provides resources on OCPD (in addition to OCD) and a directory of specialists.

Further Reading

- **Boundaries and Self-Care:**
    - *Set Boundaries, Find Peace: A Guide to Reclaiming Yourself* by Nedra Glover Tawwab.
    - *The Disease to Please: Curing the People-Pleasing Syndrome* by Harriet B. Braiker.
- **Understanding OCPD and Rigidity:**
    - *Too Perfect: When Being in Control Gets Out of Control* by Allan E. Mallinger and Jeannette Dewyze.
    - *The Perfectionist's Handbook* by Jeff Szymanski.
- **Emotional Abuse and High Conflict:**
    - *The Verbally Abusive Relationship* by Patricia Evans.
    - *Coercive Control: How Men Entrap Women in Personal Life* by Evan Stark.

- *Splitting: Protecting Yourself While Divorcing Someone with Borderline or Narcissistic Personality Disorder* by Bill Eddy and Randi Kreger.

Crisis and Abuse Resources (USA)

- **National Domestic Violence Hotline:** 1-800-799-SAFE (7233) or text START to 88788. (Provides support for emotional abuse and coercive control).
- **National Suicide Prevention Lifeline:** 988.

Appendix D: A Letter to the OCPD Partner

(Should They Choose to Read It)

This letter is a template you can adapt. It is designed to communicate the impact of their behavior empathetically but firmly. Share this only if you feel safe doing so.

Dear [Partner's Name],

I am writing this letter because I care about you and our relationship, and I want to share my experience honestly, without the escalation that often happens when we talk.

I know that you value order, responsibility, and doing things the "right way." I admire your dedication and commitment.

However, your need for perfection and control often leads to behaviors that are damaging to me and our connection. When you criticize me, correct me, or insist that things must be done exactly your way, I feel invalidated, incompetent, and emotionally distant from you.

I understand that your behavior may be driven by anxiety and a desire to prevent chaos. I am not asking you to become a different person. But I am asking you to recognize the impact of your behavior on me and to work with me to create a healthier relationship.

I need to feel respected as an equal partner. I need autonomy over my own decisions. I need emotional connection and warmth.

I have started setting boundaries to protect my own well-being. These are not meant to punish or control you. They are meant to create a safe space for me in this relationship.

[Optional: List 1-2 specific boundaries here. E.g., "I will no longer engage in arguments about the correct way to do household chores."]

I hope you will consider seeking help to understand these patterns and develop strategies for managing your rigidity and anxiety. Therapy can provide tools and support for creating the kind of relationship we both deserve.

I am committed to working on this relationship, but I need your commitment as well.

With love,

[Your Name]

Reference

- American Psychiatric Association. (2022). *Diagnostic and statistical manual of mental disorders* (5th ed., text rev.).

- Beck, A. T., Davis, D. D., & Freeman, A. (Eds.). (2015). *Cognitive therapy of personality disorders* (3rd ed.). Guilford Press.

- Diedrich, A., & Voderholzer, U. (2015). Obsessive-compulsive personality disorder: A current review. *Current Psychiatry Reports, 17*(2), 2.

- Eddy, B. (2011). *High conflict people in legal disputes*. Janis Publications.

- Freyd, J. J. (1997). Violations of power, adaptive blindness, and betrayal trauma theory. *Feminism & Psychology, 7*(1), 22–32.

- Gabbard, G. O. (2014). *Psychodynamic psychiatry in clinical practice* (5th ed.). American Psychiatric Publishing.

- Gottman, J. M., & Silver, N. (2015). *The seven principles for making marriage work: A practical guide from the country's foremost relationship expert* (Revised ed.). Harmony Books.

- Greenberg, L. S., & Safran, J. D. (1987). *Emotion in psychotherapy: Affect, cognition, and the process of change*. Guilford Press.

- Linehan, M. M. (1993). *Cognitive-behavioral treatment of borderline personality disorder*. Guilford Press.

- Maslach, C., & Jackson, S. E. (1981). The measurement of experienced burnout. *Journal of Occupational Behaviour, 2*(2), 99–113.

- Pinto, A., Steinglass, J. E., & Columbia-Suicide-QB. (2014). Obsessive-compulsive personality disorder. In J. M. Oldham, A. E. Skodol, & D. S. Bender (Eds.), *The American Psychiatric Publishing textbook of personality disorders* (2nd ed., pp. 333–354). American Psychiatric Publishing.

- Sarkis, S. A. (2018). *Gaslighting: Recognize manipulative and emotionally abusive people—and break free*. Da Capo Lifelong Books.

- Schnarch, D. M. (1997). *Passionate marriage: Keeping love and intimacy alive in committed relationships*. W. W. Norton & Company.

- Stark, E. (2007). *Coercive control: How men entrap women in personal life*. Oxford University Press.

- Tawwab, N. G. (2021). *Set boundaries, find peace: A guide to reclaiming yourself*. TarcherPerigee.

- Torgersen, S., Lygren, S., Oien, P. A., Skre, I., Onstad, S., Edvardsen, J., Tambs, K., & Kringlen, E. (2000). A twin study of personality disorders. *Comprehensive Psychiatry, 41*(6), 416–425.

- Van der Kolk, B. A. (2014). *The body keeps the score: Brain, mind, and body in the healing of trauma*. Viking.

- Walker, P. (2013). *Complex PTSD: From surviving to thriving: A guide and map for recovering from childhood trauma*. Azure Coyote.

www.ingramcontent.com/pod-product-compliance
Lightning Source LLC
LaVergne TN
LVHW051246080426
835513LV00016B/1765